ASH WINS IT ALL

ADAPTED BY JEANETTE LANE

SCHOLASTIC INC.

ISBN: 978-93-5954-767-1
First edition, 2024
This Reprint Edition, April 2026

Printed in India at MicroPrints India, New Delhi

CHAPTER ONE

"It's the Pokémon World Coronation Series Masters Eight Tournament!" The familiar voice of the Wyndon Stadium announcer filled the arena. *"The final round!"*

The stands were full of excited fans. The road to this ultimate match had been a long one. Months of battles and training had led to this opportunity, and the spectators expected an amazing head-to-head battle between two exceptional Pokémon Trainers.

"This tournament is a gathering of Champions from all over the world, a historical rarity. Both of our finalists are here after defeating an incredibly strong lineup of opponents," the announcer declared, his every word ringing with anticipation. *"And soon, they*

will clash on this field, leaving only one to stand as the pinnacle of Pokémon Trainers!"

The crowd cheered. Above the tiers of bleachers, a massive screen showed pictures of all the Trainers who had qualified for the Masters Eight. But only two were still lit up, because only two remained in the tournament: Ash Ketchum and the reigning Monarch, Leon.

In a locker room not far away, Ash was about to give one of the most important pep talks of his entire Pokémon training career, but he wasn't sure how to begin. He tightened his wristbands and stood up, making a fist. He looked around at the Pokémon who

had been on this World Coronation Series journey with him.

"Hey, guys," Ash said, his voice full of energy. "You ready?"

Pikachu, Dragonite, Lucario, Gengar, Dracovish, and Sirfetch'd all looked back at him. They were his team, and they were ready to give it their all!

"Then let's do this!" Ash exclaimed, punching his fist forward.

"Pikachu!" Pikachu jumped onto his shoulder and made the same punching motion. So fierce and adorable! Pikachu had been the best partner a Trainer could hope for.

Ash couldn't even believe that this was it: this day, this battle, this moment. Everything had led up to this opportunity to show what he and his loyal Pokémon could do—together.

With grunts of agreement, each Pokémon put its hand, paw, fin, or wing into the center of the huddle to meet Ash's own fist.

"We're gonna win! Right?!" Ash cried.

The whole crew yelled out in agreement. Arms and fins and wings raised, they cheered together! They were in it to win it!

All at once, an Eevee and a Piplup ran into the locker room and jumped into the middle of the huddle. Where did these Pokémon come from?

Then Ash saw some familiar faces. "Dawn! Chloe!" His friends had surprised him!

"Hi there, Ash!" Dawn said with a chipper wave.

Chloe gave a shy smile. "Sorry to barge in!"

Dawn had been one of Ash and Pikachu's traveling companions, and they'd shared many adventures. Chloe was a childhood friend of Goh's, and she had gotten to know Ash better since he'd signed on to work with her dad at his Pokémon laboratory.

"We'll both cheer for you," Chloe promised. "And since Goh couldn't make it, I'll be cheering on his behalf, too."

Chloe must have known how hard it was for Ash to be battling Leon without Goh there for support. After all, Goh had been with him every step of the way. It had been Goh who had first told Ash about the tournament! Goh had even been with Ash the very first time he had met Leon, after the previous year's World Coronation Series final. He had helped Ash locate new battles, supported his training, and convinced him that a string of losses did not mean that all hope was lost. He'd been there for Ash's reunion with Iris at the Opelucid City Gym, all his battles with the fierce Fighting-type Trainer Bea, and much, much more.

Despite all this, Goh had a very good reason for not being in the stadium for the finals. Since his earliest days as a Trainer, Goh had been fascinated with the Pokémon Mew. The elusive Mythical Pokémon had spurred Goh's passion for researching and capturing Pokémon. Now, Goh had earned a spot on an elite team that had assembled to study Mew—and just the day before, the project leader had called Goh in for a special mission to find Mew. Goh couldn't miss that chance!

Because of their deep connection, Ash understood why Goh couldn't pass up the opportunity. He knew Goh was there in spirit. Before they'd parted, they had promised each other one thing: "The next time we meet, we will both be smiling."

Even without Goh, Ash felt good hearing support from friends and knowing they'd be in the stands.

He replied to Chloe, "Awesome. Thanks a lot!"

"Besides . . ." Chloe added, lifting up her Evolution Pokémon, "I wanted to let Eevee see a live tournament!"

"Eevee!"

Because Eevee are able to evolve into eight different Pokémon, Chloe was always trying to expand her Eevee's horizons, to help it decide on its next Evolution.

Dawn agreed that there was something special about watching a battle live. She'd seen most of the tournament on TV. "But I had to be here for this!" she said.

For Ash, it was kind of weird to think about people from all over watching the tournament.

"Everyone is cheering for you back at the lab!" Chloe assured Ash. "Give it your all, okay?" She gave a kind smile, and Ash agreed with a nod and a determined grunt.

In another part of the stadium, Leon was also preparing for his final battle of the tournament. He had been the top-ranked Trainer for the entire season. He sat on a bench and took deep breaths, readying himself. He already had on his trademark maroon cape and baseball cap.

His younger brother, Hop, was with him.

"Lee, what's wrong?" he asked.

"Feeling nervous, but in a good way," Leon admitted. His eyes were closed, and a vision from the past

flashed through his mind: himself as a purple-haired kid, competing with a Charmander against a young girl with red hair. "I wonder . . . Why am I remembering my very first Pokémon battle now?" It made him smile.

CHAPTER TWO

The mood was very different in the actual arena. Fireworks were going off overhead, and the fans were screaming with anticipation.

"Soon we'll be introducing the two Pokémon Trainers who are aiming for the top position," the Wyndon Stadium announcer told the crowd.

In the stands, Chloe and Dawn had great seats. "You are just so cute!" Chloe said to Piplup, who was wearing a cheer uniform and shaking pom-poms. Eevee shook a pom-pom with its tail, too. They were all ready to root for their old friend Ash!

Even Team Rocket was there! They were posing as a broadcast team in order to be part of the action.

"Who'd have thought that the twerp would have

made it this far?" Jessie wondered out loud.

"Don't forget what we're here for," Meowth said, scowling. "Today we're gonna grab Pokémon who have the perfect power for Team Rocket!"

"That slipped my mind!" Jessie admitted. "And if we can't steal them, then we can't complete our mission!"

"And now let's bring out our finalists to the field!" the announcer said. *"Ranked eighth in the Masters Eight . . . The very first Champion of the Alola region . . . And hailing from Kanto . . . Ash Ketchum!"*

Ash appeared through the arena doors. He was dressed in his typical red baseball cap, blue vest, short-sleeved shirt, shorts, and sneakers. He looked like he always did. Pikachu trotted by his side.

The crowd was out of control cheering for Ash, yelling at the top of their lungs!

"Go get 'em!"

"Yeah!"

"Go, Ash!"

"We're with you all the way!"

"If Ash can't do it, no one can! Yeah! YEAH!" Dawn added her chants to the uproar.

Eevee chirped with excitement.

James tried to talk to Meowth's camera but gave up when the cheers were too loud.

"We've gotta cheer on the twerp!" Meowth agreed.

Even Wobbuffet was on board. Ash's former enemies somehow found themselves now rooting for their pesky nemesis. It was hard not to admire Ash's persistence *and* his accomplishments.

The stadium was full, but there were even more fans who were watching the final across the Pokémon world, at viewing parties or on their own—including some people who had been in the championship themselves.

"Ever since Ash entered the World Coronation Series, he has taken on and defeated a long list of powerful opponents!" the announcer told the adoring crowd. *"Perhaps the most watched contestant, he even defeated the Hoenn Champion, Steven Stone."* The announcer paused for effect. The entire crowd certainly knew what a skilled competitor Steven Stone was. *"Ash then took on the Sinnoh Champion, Cynthia, and emerged victorious! He has used Dynamax, Z-Moves, and Mega Evolution, combining them with a Pokémon battling style all his own. So what kind of inspired moves will he make today?!"*

As Ash walked out onto the arena floor, his expression was steady, but he felt his nerves exploding inside. Those last two competition battles had not been easy. Ash had fought his way back in those matches after falling behind. It had taken all his cunning and

strategy to beat Steven and Cynthia. What would he do if Leon took the lead today? Would he have what it takes to defeat the tournament's current champion?

"Now, the Trainer facing Ash . . ." the announcer began.

But did Leon really need an introduction? Leon was the reigning world champion, undefeated since his last tournament win! He was not only superb in the battling arena, he was also a force for good in the greater Pokémon community. He had even taken Ash under his wing, training with him and combining forces to help topple an evil plot by Chairman Rose.

The Wyndon Stadium announcer tried to put

Leon's achievements into words. *"He's the reigning Monarch, with worldwide name recognition. He's the role model and battling goal for Pokémon Trainers all over the globe!"* The announcer's pitch rose with each word. He couldn't pump any more praise or energy into his introduction. *"Ranked number one in the Masters Eight . . . The Champion of the Galar region . . . Leon!"*

Leon strode into the arena, his cape flapping behind him. He was so calm, so composed. He looked like he'd done all this before—because he had! But he had never faced Ash in an arena battle. Every matchup was different.

Up in the stands, Leon's brother, Hop, cheered with all his might. "Do it, Lee!"

Just then, a familiar face appeared by him. "Hop?"

"Sonia! So glad you came!" Hop enthused.

Here were two of the few people who knew Leon beyond his battling record. They both understood that Leon was human, like everyone else. Sonia had been friends with Leon since before he had discovered battling. And through shared work researching Pokémon and Dynamaxing, Sonia had also developed a friendship with Ash and Goh.

She understood how important this battle was to both Leon and Ash, and she admired each of them. She would be cheering for a great match in which both competitors felt good about their effort and that of their Pokémon.

"Better to see this in person!" Sonia said to Hop.

"Now, can Ash manage to put an end to Leon's unbeaten winning streak?" the announcer questioned. *"Or will Leon renew his title of being perpetually undefeated?"* The crowd's cheers grew even louder as the announcer got even more dramatic. *"This is truly the ultimate battle!"*

Leon took a powerful stance. "Ash! So we meet again!" he said. "This time on the field."

It was kind of a funny thing for Leon to say—after all, the two had seen each other on that very field just the day before. Leon had wanted to talk with Ash and Goh about something very different from the tournament—about the Legendary Pokémon, Eternatus—but that discussion was far from their minds now. They were both focused on one thing.

"Right!" Ash agreed. "Also, in the finals!" He pounded his fist into his other hand. This was the moment Ash had been waiting for. This was it!

"It's the best stage possible!" Leon raised his arms above his head, motioning to the stands full of fans. "And the one who's been looking forward to this battle the most . . ." Leon declared with a grin, "is me!"

Ash grunted. He knew better than to argue with the champ.

"Pika," Pikachu added with determination.

It was bizarre for Ash to think of Leon anticipating a battle with him. Ash still felt like a newcomer to this level of competing. But he had more experience than people realized. He had been focused on Pokémon and nothing but Pokémon for years! He approached battling unlike anyone else. He focused on his bond with his Pokémon, and that gave him an edge.

Still, Leon was no slouch. He wasn't in it just to win it. It was Sonia who had told Ash about Leon as a little kid. Pokémon had given Leon direction, a focus, a mission.

"It's Ash and the Champion on equal ground," observed Professor Oak, watching them on TV all the way back in Kanto. "Look how much Ash has grown." The professor had every reason to be proud. After all, he was Ash's first mentor. Professor Oak had been there when Ash had first met Pikachu! If it had

not been for Professor Oak, would Ash and Pikachu even be in the World Coronation Series?

Sitting next to the professor was another of Ash and Pikachu's biggest fans. "Yes!" cheered Delia, Ash's loving mother. "Trust in your Pokémon and do your best! Go, Ash!" From the very beginning, Delia had been supportive of Ash and his intense interest in Pokémon. She had allowed his passion to take him on journeys all around the world. She was with Professor Oak in Pallet Town, gathered with Ash's menagerie of Pokémon around them on the grassy lawn. They were all focused on the broadcast of the match, all cheering for Ash.

CHAPTER THREE

Back in the stadium, Dan took his job as the arena referee very seriously. Balancing on his deluxe hoverboard far above the arena floor, he made sure everyone was aware of the official rules. "The finals consist of a six-on-six Full Battle," Dan began. "There will be no limits on time or switching out Pokémon. The one who leaves all six of their opponent's Pokémon unable to battle wins!" Dan stared down at the Trainers. "Also, a contestant is only permitted to use Dynamax, a Z-Move, or Mega Evolution once per—"

"Hold it!" Leon interrupted.

Ash's jaw dropped. Both he and Dan looked at the Champion in shock. This was unexpected.

"Leon?" Dan asked, zooming down to be closer to the contestants.

"Just once is pretty boring," Leon declared. "So come at me using them all, okay?"

Ash tried to process what Leon was saying. "Really?" he asked.

"This is the ultimate test of an all-out competition!" Leon exclaimed. "Dynamax, Z-Moves, and Mega Evolution! I want to battle against all of them, and *beat* them all! What about you? Don't you want to see a full-power battle?"

The crowd cheered—this could be the most epic battle ever! In the stands, Sonia laughed. She recognized this Leon. She was happy to see her old friend full of energy and ambition. And she could see that Leon wasn't proposing an all-out battle

just to win—he wanted to be *part* of the ultimate battle. Leon was in it for the experience, for the fun.

"Go, Lee!" cried Hop. "Yeah! That's my brother with the awesome ideas!"

Chloe was concerned about Ash and how this rule change might affect his chances for success. "What does that mean?" she asked Dawn.

"It means it will be an amazing match!" Dawn said. She called, "All right, you can do it, Ash!"

Dan held a hand to his earpiece. "The officials in charge of the World Coronation Series have agreed to Leon's suggestion!" he announced, then turned toward Ash. "Ash, do you agree?"

Ash replied without hesitation, "You bet! Sounds awesome!"

"Pika," Ash's partner agreed. They each raised a fist with certainty.

The crowd went wild! They were about to witness history!

"This is unprecedented!" the announcer cried, making certain that everyone in the stadium realized that they were about to see something brand-new.

Cynthia and Diantha, both semifinalists who had been in the tournament, were watching this matchup together from a sofa in one of the stadium's luxury boxes, high above the battlefield. Within the privacy

of the box, they would be better able to share their insights about the match.

Cynthia smirked. "That's something Leon would do," she said.

"Yes," Diantha agreed. She had been the most recent Trainer to fall to Leon's dominance. "This may be the kind of battle we'll never see again."

Back on the field, Dan directed Ash and Leon. "Send your Pokémon to the field!" he said. "Three, two, and one . . . Go!"

"Now, Pikachu, I choose you!" Ash cried out. He didn't need to throw out a Poké Ball, since Pikachu had refused to go in one since their early days together. Instead, Pikachu stood at Ash's side, even when it was not battling. That was just one piece of Ash and Pikachu's special understanding, their teamwork, their partnership.

"Come on out, Cinderace!" Leon called, pitching a Poké Ball to the center of the stadium floor. The Striker Pokémon came out in fighting mode, bobbing and weaving like a boxer in a ring.

"I'm counting on you!" Ash told Pikachu as the Electric type bounded to the center of the arena floor. "I want you to be the first on the field!"

"Pikachuuuu," his partner responded, sparks crackling from its cheeks.

"Are you saying you don't care about strategies?" Leon asked Ash. Leon clearly felt like it was a mistake for Ash to lead with his heart—with Pikachu. "Let's shut them down, Cinderace!" he yelled.

"Cinda," Cinderace responded, its fists raised as it bounced from foot to foot. Leon had made his message clear: attack early and attack fast.

Up in the stands, Hop said to Sonia, "Cinderace is Leon's number-one striker."

"Battle . . . begin!" Dan declared.

And just like that, it started! As the crowd roared, Ash shouted over the cheers, "Thunderbolt!"

Pikachu leaped into the air, lightning buzzing all around.

"Use Scorching Sands!" Leon directed.

Cinderace threw itself into a jumping spin, striking the ground, and a ball of swirling sand appeared. Cinderace rose into the air and kicked the whirling ball right at Pikachu.

"Pika-chuuuuuuuu!" Pikachu landed the Thunderbolt and ricocheted to the ground just as Cinderace's move came in for a hit.

"Cinderace and Pikachu's attacks were like cross-counters!" the announcer called out.

"What?!" Ash shouted, uncertain what had happened. Cinderace seemed unaffected.

"Scorching Sands is a Ground-type attack that's super effective against Pikachu!" the announcer observed. *"Meanwhile, Cinderace is unscathed after the Thunderbolt attack."*

Pikachu stood on the battlefield, panting. Ash sensed something was not right.

"Ash, are you familiar with the Libero Ability?" Leon asked his younger, less experienced opponent.

"Libero?" Ash repeated, feeling confused. Pikachu was gritting its teeth, trying to recover.

"That's right. When Cinderace attacks, it becomes the same type as its move," Leon explained.

"That means that Cinderace is now a Ground type?" Ash replied, still uncertain.

"Pika," Pikachu muttered with frustration.

"Pikachu, return!" Ash declared.

"Pika?" Pikachu turned to look at Ash. Should it really return so soon?

All the spectators were trying to process this new information as well. Even the other members of the Masters Eight knew this was a significant tactic for Leon to pull at the start.

"If Electric-type attacks won't work . . ." Cynthia began.

". . . There's not much else Ash and Pikachu can do," Diantha finished.

As an Electric type, Pikachu did not have much power against a Ground type. That was a basic of Pokémon battling. Under normal circumstances, Cinderace was a Fire type, but Ash realized that he couldn't count on things to be normal against a pro like Leon. This was the finals—there was nothing normal about that.

CHAPTER FOUR

Ash realized Leon had thwarted his main plan, which was to start with his prime partner. As Pikachu reached the sideline, Ash knelt down. “You all right?” he asked.

“Pika pika.” Pikachu looked up at Ash. It seemed to be in good spirits even though it would have to wait its turn.

“Okay. Watch everyone else battle,” Ash replied, then turned his attention to Leon.

“Cinderace, return!” Leon directed. “Inteleon, let’s go!”

Everyone watching was surprised that he was switching out Pokémon so soon.

“Gengar, I choose you!” Ash decided.

“All right!” Leon yelled. “Use Snipe Shot!” Inteleon

pointed its finger at Gengar and released the Water-type move.

"Shadow Ball!" Ash countered.

Inteleon's shot hit Gengar in the eye, but Gengar recovered and whirled a giant, glowing, purple Shadow Ball right at Inteleon.

"Knock it down," Leon directed, which Inteleon did with one swipe of its tail.

The outcome surprised Ash and Pikachu. Inteleon made it look so easy!

"Use Dark Pulse," Leon commanded, continuing his attack. Inteleon conjured an aura ball that floated at the end of its long, thin finger. The move's damage

came from a surge of dark thoughts that exploded from the ball on impact.

"Gengar, dodge it!" cried Ash.

At once, Gengar used it powers to make an escape into the ground of the stadium, so Inteleon's Dark Pulse missed. Ash thought it was a clever move, but Leon did not look impressed.

"Pointless," Leon said, still full of confidence. "Use Aqua Jet!"

Water surged from Inteleon's three-toed feet, and the Secret Agent Pokémon began to spin. The water shot up around it like a fountain until its swirling speed turned the water into a giant spiral

that kept expanding across the battleground.

"What is that?" Ash wondered.

"Is that a Counter Shield?" Dawn said from her spot up in the stands. Piplup seemed worried. They could really see the force of the water.

"That twirling battle tactic looks just like what Pikachu did in the semifinals!" the announcer pointed out.

Leon smirked. "You see, that move was just too much fun, so I decided to borrow it from you."

"That's great," Ash replied sarcastically. How had Leon mastered it so quickly?

Gengar attempted to emerge from the arena floor but kept getting bashed by the constant powerful surges of water from Inteleon. Gengar finally got to its feet with a grunt, doing its best to hop over the pinwheel of water crashing around the arena.

"Surprise! How does it feel?" Leon asked with a chuckle, giving Ash a taste of his own medicine.

Ash clenched his fists. "It wipes away any place to hide . . ." he thought out loud, trying to find a solution.

Up in their viewing box, Cynthia and Diantha watched with great interest. Ash had used that move

on Cynthia in their battle, so she knew how it felt. "The pressure is really on for Ash, huh?" Cynthia said.

"Yes," Diantha agreed.

Ash came to a decision. "Gengar, use Will-O-Wisp!" he called. Gengar boosted itself into the air and shot out a multipronged Fire-type move that stopped the watery spiral with several bright purple explosions.

"Watch out, Inteleon!" Leon warned.

Gengar's move left a smoky cloud in the arena. Through the haze, Ash yelled, "Gengar, return!" He grabbed a Poké Ball. "Let's do this . . . big time!"

"It's coming . . ." Leon murmured with enthusiasm, making a fist.

"Gigantamax, go!" Ash cried. The Poké Ball glowed

hot pink and grew larger in his palm before he threw it toward the sky.

Gengar's Gigantamax form was epic. It was otherworldly. The oversized purple Pokémon pulled itself up from the ground, out of a black chasm that seemed to snap, crackle, and pop with power.

"Ash is using Gigantamax right here and now!" the announcer exclaimed, unable to contain his own excitement. *"How is Leon planning to counter it?"*

Leon's request to allow for Dynamax, Z-Moves, and Mega Evolution at any time was already changing the strategies for this final round of the World Coronation Series. Ash was bold to make the first move! How would this play out?

Gigantamax Gengar took up most of its side of the playing field. It roared, its mouth as wide and deep as a cave. The entire stadium shook.

"Use Snipe Shot!" Leon yelled.

Inteleon aimed with both its pointer fingers.

"Oh my. A double?" Sonia said in the stands.

Leon's little brother beamed. "Lee's Inteleon is able to shoot using both hands!" Twice the power!

"G-Max Terror!" Ash directed. Not only would Gigantamax Gengar's move prevent its opponent from

switching out, it also caused huge objects—like a teakettle or chair—to appear and hurl toward the opponent. Gengar's objects whizzed across the battlefield, right at Inteleon.

"In-te-le-on." Inteleon grunted as it zapped each item that came its way. Then it zapped Gigantamax Gengar right on its very large forehead. Gengar's whole body shook with the shock.

"Both of them are taking plenty of damage!" the announcer explained.

The Trainers watched as their moves played out. Both were pleased.

"As an aftereffect of G-Max Terror, Leon can't

switch out his Pokémon!" the announcer reminded everyone.

"Use Dark Pulse!" Leon called out to Inteleon.

"Max Ooze, go!" called Ash. In an instant, Gigantamax Gengar released a wave of purple sludge that sloshed over the arena floor. "Gengar, go full power!"

The Shadow Pokémon kept the ooze flowing, targeting Inteleon with splashy strikes. Inteleon tried to dodge the slush, but the stadium became a lake of purple.

"Strike it down!" Leon yelled. Inteleon leaped up and set off two powerful pulses while twisting through the air. The pulses went straight into Gigantamax Gengar's gullet!

But before Inteleon landed, a nasty blast of Max Ooze power slammed it in the back and threw it across the stadium floor. A direct hit!

"Inteleon!" Leon cried out.

"I don't know if it's the result of Dark Pulse's direct hit, but Gengar has returned to normal size," the announcer observed.

Dan swooped in on his hoverboard to make his first call of the match. "Inteleon is unable to battle. The first to score in the finals is Ash!"

CHAPTER FIVE

"All right!" Ash gave a shout for himself, pumping both fists in the air. He had scored!

"Pika pika!" Pikachu cheered and leaped.

Up in the stands, Hop was disappointed and shocked.

But in another part of the stadium, Chloe and Dawn were thrilled! Eevee and Piplup shook their pom-poms in delight.

Ash's friends around the world were rooting for him. "And he scores!" Professor Oak cheered back at his lab.

Beside the professor, Delia watched with motherly pride. "Gengy really worked quite hard for that!" she said. Ash's Pokémon who were back at the lab shared in the celebration as well.

Even Team Rocket couldn't contain their excitement. Ash might have been their longtime nemesis, but that relationship brought Team Rocket closer to Ash's greatness. "We're moving on up!" James chanted.

"Monarch, schmonarch!" Jessie teased. "Leon's finding out the power of a twerp!"

Ash wasn't just any twerp—he was Team Rocket's twerp, and they wouldn't let anyone forget it!

"You all right, Gengar?" Ash asked.

Gengar twirled with glee. *"Gen-gar!"*

"Inteleon, return!" Leon stated, holding out a Poké Ball. "You made this easier," he said to it in the ball. "We'll win! I'll be catching up soon enough. You'll see!"

That made Ash flinch a little. Leon was so confident!

"A fire got lit under Leon," Sonia observed to Hop. "And when he's like this, he's amazing!" She leaned forward in anticipation.

Leon cried, "Let's go! Now, Mr. Rime!"

If Goh had been in attendance that day, he would have done what he always did when a new Pokémon took the battle stage: He'd use his Pokédex to learn more about it. He'd have found out that Mr. Rime is a dual Ice- and Psychic-type Pokémon that hails from the Galar region, and that it releases psychic power from the pattern on its belly.

Leon's Mr. Rime came out of its Poké Ball tap-dancing! Its belly looked like a face, and it spun its cane of ice so fast that it looked like a propeller.

Ash wasn't sure what to expect. "Use Sludge Bomb!" he yelled to Gengar, who sent a squadron of bombs through the air.

"Use Freeze-Dry!" Leon called to Mr. Rime, who shot a freezing blast at the bombs.

"That Sludge Bomb just completely froze up!" the announcer said, surprised. Then the whole floor of the battleground crystallized into a sheet of ice. Mr. Rime had quite a few tricks up those suit sleeves!

"Mr. Rime, Freeze-Dry!" Leon repeated the move, but something stopped his Pokémon from following through. Mr. Rime kept aiming its cane at Gengar, but nothing happened.

"It looks like Mr. Rime can't use its moves!" the announcer exclaimed.

"Is that the Cursed Body Ability?" Leon asked Ash.

"Yeah, you can't use Freeze-Dry for a while," Ash explained.

"You thought that would help you?" Leon questioned with a chuckle.

The ice on the arena floor started creeping up Gengar's body—soon the Pokémon was encased in ice!

"Gengar is now frozen stiff because of Freeze-Dry's

frightening power!" the announcer pointed out.

"No way!" Ash cried.

"Pika!" Pikachu fretted.

"Use Psychic Terrain!" Leon said, knowing it was a power move, especially when Gengar was already down.

Mr. Rime's eyes shone a brilliant yellow as the move took effect. There was something spooky about Mr. Rime and its face, which showed very little expression. It seemed to be as cold as ice in its moves and its moods.

"Psychic Terrain is activated! With this, the power of the Psychic-type attacks is increased!" the announcer told the crowd.

Ash and Pikachu both let out startled yelps as a pale purple dome appeared over the field of play.

"With this, the battlefield now becomes a battle *stage* for Mr. Rime!" Leon announced with enthusiasm. "Expanding Force!"

Ash gasped. "Gengar, no!" Expanding Force was, indeed, a Psychic-type attack. Therefore, Mr. Rime became even more powerful. The Pokémon seemed to glide over the battlefield like a graceful, menacing ice-skater.

Ash was a little rattled. He hadn't expected Leon to use a Psychic-type Pokémon so early in their match!

Mr. Rime slid right up to Gengar and touched its cane to the ice that was encapsulating Gengar. With a pulse of psychic power, the cane shattered the ice and sent Gengar flying.

"Gengar is unable to battle," Dan declared.

Ash and Leon were even once again. There were mixed reactions all over the stadium.

"Well, all right!" Hop yelled with both excitement and relief.

"The twerp got outclassed," Meowth said with a sneer. Leon truly was displaying the tactical brilliance of a reigning Monarch.

"Gengar, return!" Ash stated. "You did an awesome job!"

"Pika," Pikachu reassured both Gengar and Ash.

"Inteleon, I declare this your win!" Leon bellowed, one arm raised in the air. "Its valiant efforts were what made it all possible." Leon glanced across the arena to see Ash's reaction. "You understand it as well. What's most important in a Full Battle is that the damage done by one Pokémon leads to the next victory. The *overall* win comes from the whole team!"

Ash knew that. Of course he did! But the way Leon said it felt very pointed. It felt as if Leon was trying to teach Ash a lesson. Leon was still playing a psychic game, and not just with his Psychic-type Pokémon!

Ash needed to stay strong and believe in himself and his Pokémon, or this battle was already lost. After all, this was the stage of dreams, where the strongest Trainer would be determined!

Both Trainers had five remaining Pokémon. Leon still had Mr. Rime in play.

"The ground is covered in ice and Psychic Terrain . . ." Ash mumbled to himself.

"So tell me, Ash. Which Pokémon will you choose next?" Leon prompted.

Ash clenched his fists in frustration. Maybe it wasn't such a good thing that he and Leon knew each other so well. "Sirfetch'd! I choose you!" Ash yelled.

"A Fighting type?" Leon asked, sounding doubtful.

In the safety and comfort of the skybox, Cynthia also had her doubts. "Against a Psychic type like Mr. Rime, Sirfetch'd is at a disadvantage," she observed.

The matchup didn't stop Ash's fans from cheering. "Go, Ash! Go, Sirfetch'd! Get 'em now!" Dawn cried. Beside her, Chloe quietly willed Ash to win.

"'Kay, Sirfetch'd, there's something only you can do. Got it?" Ash directed.

Sirfetch'd gave a nod to show it understood.

"Use Fury Cutter!" Ash cried.

With a backswing of its leek, Sirfetch'd initiated the move. It held its leafy shield up as a defense, and its leek glowed a neon green.

Mr. Rime glided with ease over the ice and aimed its cane like a sword as it reached Sirfetch'd.

Sirfetch'd swung with smaller strikes and then, gaining speed and power, unleashed bigger swings.

Mr. Rime parried the jabs away with its icicle cane, again and again.

Team Rocket joined the roar of the crowd. "Swing that leek like a saxophone!" James yelled.

"For Gengar!" Meowth added. Meowth seemed to understand what Leon had been preaching: that the

efforts of all the Pokémon on the team were connected. Sirfetch'd would want to deal some damage to Mr. Rime as a way of redeeming Gengar's defeat. Of course.

Sirfetch'd put all its might into the fight and landed a strike right between Mr. Rime's jacket buttons! The jab propelled Mr. Rime into the air and then across the ice.

"It's a direct hit with Fury Cutter, which is super effective against Psychic types," the announcer pointed out. It seemed to have been a good move, but who knew what Leon had planned next!

"Brutal Swing, let's go!" Ash yelled.

Sirfetch'd began to spin until it was a blurry whirl. It spun at Mr. Rime like a high-speed top.

"Stop them in their tracks!" Leon directed.

Mr. Rime showed no emotion on its actual face, but eerily, the face pattern on its belly appeared to be laughing. Then Mr. Rime grabbed the Wild Duck Pokémon's leek between its two hands.

The applause from the crowd seemed to fade out as everyone watched.

"Expanding Force!" Leon shouted, and a purple glow of energy came from Mr. Rime's belly pattern.

Sirfetch'd covered its head with its leafy shield, but the energy was too strong. A powerful beam shot up from below, crackling with yellow and blue sparks. The surge flung Sirfetch'd across the arena. It landed with a thud, its shield rattling to a stop several feet away.

Pikachu flinched at the blow to its beaked buddy.

"This time, Sirfetch'd *was hit with a super-effective attack!"* the announcer stated, sounding a little shaken himself. *"The combination of Psychic Terrain and Expanding Force is exceptionally powerful!"*

"Sirfetch'd, you all right?" Ash asked.

Noble as always, Sirfetch'd sat up and grunted a reply. It had taken the hit well.

“Use Triple Axel!” yelled Leon. Mr. Rime executed this Ice-type move, spinning through the air and kicking Sirfetch’d not once, not twice, but three times!

Sirfetch’d still was not down for the count, though its shield was across the arena.

“Expanding Force!” Leon declared. The Monarch just kept calling for it, and Mr. Rime just kept bringing it.

Ash did his best to counter the onslaught. “Use Detect!”

Sirfetch’d skirted the attack, flinging itself into the air with its leek.

“Get your shield! Go!” Ash yelled. Sirfetch’d launched itself into the air with its leek and sailed over Mr. Rime.

"It's flying!" the announcer exclaimed.

"It's stunning!" Chloe and Dawn said in awe.

Even Hop was impressed.

"So, you're pole-vaulting?" Leon said, amused by the Pokémon's creative problem-solving. "Then, for our move . . . Use Triple Axel!"

Sirfetch'd grabbed its shield just in time to block the impact of this Triple Axel.

"Use Fury Cutter!" Ash yelled.

"Here it comes, Mr. Rime," warned Leon, who was clearly enjoying the antics of the matchup.

"It's time to cut . . . the . . . field!" Ash declared.

Instead of taking its leek to the air, Sirfetch'd began to strike the ice on the arena floor, again and again. *"Sirrrrrr-fetccchhhh'd!"* the Pokémon screeched as it aimed at the ground. With each hit from Sirfetch'd, the ice cracked more.

"The energy of Psychic Terrain has been eliminated!" the announcer explained.

"That's the way, Sirfetch'd!" Ash congratulated his Pokémon on a job well done. Sirfetch'd took a noble pose. That said, the battle was far from won.

Leon was putting together what had just happened. "So that's the reason . . ."

"Since it's a Bug-type move, it's capable of destroying a Psychic-type move," Diantha deduced up in the skybox. The complexities of the moves and power plays were tricky to understand, even for the most accomplished Trainers!

Chloe was playing catch-up on the strategy as well. "I guess not all moves are meant to attack other Pokémon," she said, impressed that Ash had figured out a way to bring Psychic Terrain to an end. It had really given Leon and Mr. Rime the upper hand!

"Yep, that's the way Ash rolls," Dawn confirmed.

Even though Psychic Terrain had been broken, a layer of ice still covered the battlefield.

Ash called Sirfetch'd back to its Poké Ball.

CHAPTER SIX

It was Lucario's turn.

"You're wrapping this up!" Ash said to his Pokémon.

"Be careful," Leon said to Mr. Rime. "We have no idea what it is they're planning."

Mr. Rime observed Lucario as the Fighting-type Pokémon strode forward.

"Let's go, Lucario!" Ash called out. Lucario gave a determined nod and grunted, taking a fighting stance. "Our bond of friendship," Ash called, touching the glove on his left hand. "Mega Evolve!" His voice rang out, and the transformation began.

With the aid of the Key Stone Lucarionite, Lucario and Ash were able to use Mega Evolution to increase their connection! Lucario felt a surge through its body

as the powerful bands of energy encircled it. Mega Evolution was always such a spectacle! The power of the relationship between Pokémon and Trainer magnified their battling power.

"After using Gigantamax, Ash now brings out Mega Evolution," the announcer stated. While it was thrilling for the spectators, was Ash using all his tricks too early in the match?

An iridescent glow emanated from Mega Lucario. Mega Lucario's cream fur was longer, it had spikes on its paws and feet, and it had more aura sensors. But the biggest change was in Mega Lucario's own aura. It sent energy that whipped through the whole stadium like a gusty wind.

James squinted against the energy's bright light. "Now that's lively!" he said. Jessie shielded her eyes.

"Lucario is so determined!" Chloe yelled against the gale-like force. Dawn could barely hold on to Piplup and her hat.

Even Hop was enjoying the show!

Dan, the referee, couldn't control his hoverboard as it was forced up into the open air above the arena.

"Lucario's aura is overwhelming!" the announcer said, summing it up.

As soon as things had settled, Ash was ready. "Use Bullet Punch!"

Leon countered with the reliable Triple Axel.

Mega Lucario ran at Mr. Rime with all its might, fists flying, but Mr. Rime glided out of the way.

"What an incredible dodge!" the announcer commended Leon and Mr. Rime. *"Even without Psychic Terrain, the ice gives Mr. Rime an incredible advantage!"*

Mega Lucario seemed surprised by how sprightly Mr. Rime was on the ice.

Then, with no warning, Mr. Rime came at Mega Lucario with a Triple Axel to the jaw!

"Lucario!" Ash yelled as the Fighting-type Pokémon fell to its knees.

"Pikaaaa!"

Meanwhile, Mr. Rime was skating in graceful circles like it was out for a casual stroll.

"All right, time for another Triple Axel," Leon said, and Mr. Rime leaped into action, making impact with each rotation.

Panting, Lucario stared down at the ice. It didn't feel its best, but it wasn't done.

"So, it endured that," Leon observed. "That's Mega Evolution for you!"

"Lucario!" Ash called with fresh energy. "Let's use your aura!"

Lucario perked up. It took a deep breath, raised its chin, and closed its eyes. Almost immediately, its aura

energy was visible—waves of violet and turquoise that rose from Lucario like flames. The aura emanated all around its body like an iridescent force field.

"Now feel its movements. Just like that!" Ash directed. "Build up more aura!" Ash tried to focus everything he had on Lucario in that moment. A sphere of aura began to build between Mega Lucario's paws.

"I like it," Leon mused. "Let me see if you can sense Mr. Rime! Use Triple Axel!"

Mr. Rime was at the far end of the arena when Leon called for the damage-dealing move. Mr. Rime began building up speed, skating toward Mega

Lucario. *"Rime, rime, rime,"* it said with each stroke. Mega Lucario stood motionless, its eyes still closed. Mr. Rime rose into the air, entering its twisting jump. Without opening its eyes, Mega Lucario ducked out of the way.

"'Kay, quick! Let 'er rip!" Ash shouted, and Mega Lucario released the Aura Sphere. The electric-blue ball exploded right on Mr. Rime's backside, sending the Psychic-type Pokémon sprawling! Lucario had landed the attack using only its aura.

Dan had descended to the battlefield. "Mr. Rime is unable to battle!" he confirmed.

"You did it, Lucario!" Ash exclaimed. Pikachu cheered!

Mega Lucario was still panting, but it gave a humble smile over its shoulder. This is what they'd been training for all this time!

"It's the second of Leon's Pokémon to be eliminated," the announcer reminded everyone.

"You really made a difference, Mr. Rime," Leon said sincerely as he retrieved the Poké Ball. He then looked up. "Ash and Lucario, that was impressive!"

"Thanks, Leon," Ash replied, touching the rim of his ball cap. "I really believe in Lucario!"

CHAPTER SEVEN

Leon might have just given Ash and Lucario a genuine compliment, but in less than a blink, he was back on the offensive. Leon knew his next move. "And this one is next!" he announced. "Dragapult, now!"

"Dragapult," the Stealth Pokémon snarled as it hovered just above the playing field. Ash had encountered a Dragapult before. With its triangular head, a pair of live Dreepy missiles stored in its horns, and the ability to turn invisible, the Stealth Pokémon was not easy to forget.

"Use Double Team, let's go!" Ash said. As soon as Mega Lucario had duplicated itself again and again, Ash gave more direction. "Get in using Bullet Punch!"

The team of Lucario thundered toward Dragapult.

In the last instant, the real Lucario bounded up and unleashed a barrage of punches.

Dragapult fell to the ground, but when it rose, it was all confidence. Leon assessed Mega Lucario's attack. "Use Flamethrower!" he called.

Dragapult dropped its jaw, and a massive blaze streamed out.

Mega Lucario put its paw over its eyes as it struggled against the flames. "Lucario, return!" Ash called, deciding to make a swap. "You're up this time, Dracovish!"

"Draaa-cooo," the Fossil Pokémon mumbled as it flipped through the air and came to a landing on the battlefield.

"Look at that!" the announcer enthused. *"It's become a showdown of Dragon types."*

"Use Dragon Rush!" Ash shouted, jumping right in with Dracovish. His Pokémon darted forward with great speed.

"Use Dragon Darts!" Leon responded, taking advantage of Dragapult's Dreepy. The two small Lingering Pokémon really liked being launched out at high speeds. They raced right at Dracovish!

"Quick, stop it!" Ash yelled, but Dracovish couldn't reach Dragapult. The first Dreepy hit Dracovish in the belly, bringing it to a stop. Then the Dracovish caught the second one in its mouth. Its tail stuck out, wriggling and wriggling.

With the Dreepy still clenched in its mouth, Dracovish whimpered. Its body vibrated with each wiggle the Dreepy made. It looked back at Ash with worry.

"What's wrong?" Ash asked.

"We'll take that back, thanks!" Leon said. He sent the first Dreepy back at Dracovish to dislodge the Dreepy that was stuck. Then both Dreepy returned to their stations in Dragapult's horns. Dragapult seemed satisfied.

"You all right, Dracovish?" questioned Ash.

"Something is happening to Dracovish's body . . . What is going on?!" The announcer said, befuddled. The spikes on Dracovish's belly were surrounded by a

magenta aura. They looked twice as long as usual, and they were glowing!

"Ignore it!" Leon said to his own Dragon type. "We're going on offense!"

While Leon had a battle to consider, the spectators were free to consider Dracovish's condition. Cynthia was especially thoughtful. "The collision of Dragon-type attacks . . . It's awakened a power in Dracovish that may have been dormant for quite a long time."

"What's up next?" Diantha wondered. "How can Ash utilize this transformation?"

Ash didn't know what to do. He was worried about Dracovish, but he was also battling in the finals of the World Coronation Series. He needed a plan!

"Use Thunderbolt!" Leon yelled.

Ash watched as the move hit Dracovish with full impact.

"I was hoping to show Dragapult off," Leon said, "so let's wrap this up!" Dragapult took off, zooming headfirst toward its opponent.

"Dracovish, go!" Ash yelled.

Dracovish stayed put, but its spikes lit up again. As soon as Dragapult was within reach, the spikes wrapped around the other Dragon type. Dragapult was pinned to Dracovish's belly!

"What?" Leon said.

Pikachu gave a happy chirp.

"Well, all right!" Ash cheered, celebrating Dracovish's newfound skill. "Fishious Rend!" he called, hoping Dracovish's signature move would be enough to give it the upper hand—or fin—in this battle.

"It's putting the bite on!" the announcer said, knowing just what the move entailed. Dracovish's lower jaw dropped, then closed on the tip of Dragapult's triangular head. *"Dracovish is countering, and Dragapult can't run away!"*

"That's a lot of power," admitted Leon.

"Now it's clamping down even harder! Almost exactly like Grapploct's Octolock attack!" the announcer observed. Ash knew all about that intense move from his battles against Bea earlier in the tournament!

But Leon wasn't worried. "Careful, Ash. You really shouldn't underestimate Dragapult," he advised. "Now use Dragon Tail!"

Dragapult's tail was one of the only parts not contained by Dracovish. Its tail began to glow a brilliant green and stretched to be very long, way into the sky.

"Don't let go!" Ash called to Dracovish. "Use Ice Fang, now!"

The Ice Fang move was quick. It grew thick crystals from Dracovish's mouth down onto Dragapult's back and along its glowing tail . . . But Dragapult's long tail still was able to twist around and whip Dracovish right in the head! At once, Dracovish disappeared. It was zapped back to its Poké Ball, only to be replaced by . . . Dragonite?

"Wait, Dragonite?" Ash said, confused. Why was the Dragon Pokémon on the battlefield?

Dragonite looked as perplexed as Ash. It floated

near the center of the arena floor, its mustard-yellow wings flapping.

"It's Dragon Tail!" the announcer explained. *"It's the move that sends Pokémon flying and then forces a different Pokémon out onto the field!"*

Many spectators were surprised. "Wait, is that even possible?" Chloe asked.

"And right after Dracovish had had its awakening!" Dawn added with frustration.

Hop cheered for his brother, pumping his fist. "Lee, good going!"

CHAPTER EIGHT

"Dragapult, you're still battling a Dragon type," Leon pointed out. Apparently, Dragon Tail was such a tricky move that Leon had to update Dragapult on their battle plan. When Dragapult nodded with understanding, Leon immediately launched into a fresh attack. "Dragon Darts!"

"Fly up!" Ash said to Dragonite. "Use Dragon Dance!"

Dragonite flew straight up, whirling around like a winged cyclone. Dragonite was gaining speed with its move . . . but the Dreepy were locked onto it! They attacked, again and again, as Dragonite spun. Dragonite grunted with each hit.

From the ground, Ash tried to think of a winning move. "Use Dragon Claw!" he cried.

Dragonite stopped spinning and began to swing its paws, but the Dreepy dodged its every punch. Then, all at once, they dove down toward the ground.

"Follow them, Dragonite!" Ash rooted for his Pokémon to get on the offensive.

"Use Dragon Tail!" Leon called, again using Dragapult's trick-switch move. Dragapult whapped Dragonite. It instantly went back to its Poké Ball and was replaced in the battle by Mega Lucario.

"It must be hard for Ash to work that way," Diantha remarked from the skybox.

"Ash may have more Pokémon remaining, but Leon's the one controlling the pace," Cynthia observed. Every battle had its own vibe, depending

on the Trainers and the Pokémon involved. Trainers could only prepare so much; a lot could change within the course of the match. Ash certainly did not anticipate Leon being able to switch out which of his own Pokémon was in battle. It was a real power play!

"Pikaaa." Ash's partner let out a troubled sigh on the sideline.

"It's okay, buddy," Ash assured Pikachu. "Don't worry." Ash took deep breaths, trying to calm his own nerves. "Lucario, let's wrap this up! Use Bullet Punch!"

Lucario took off with its speed attack, only to be countered by a Thunderbolt from Dragapult.

"Reversal, go!" Ash called for the Fighting-type move instinctively. Reversal had more power when a Pokémon's energy reserves were low. It had been a real game changer for Ash and Lucario in some of their toughest matches.

Mega Lucario let out a growl of frustration.

"Use Bullet Punch!" Ash cried. Mega Lucario started to build up to the attack, but it couldn't move. Its aura seemed to fizzle as it stood there, motionless. Its face was frozen in a snarl.

"Mega Lucario has been paralyzed!" the announcer said.

Leon directed Dragapult. "Now, use Flamethrower!" Dragapult let out a blaze of flame that engulfed the other Pokémon.

At once, Lucario was transformed out of its Mega-Evolved state. It stood there for a moment before toppling backward.

Dan zoomed down on his hoverboard to offer the voice of the doomed. "Lucario is unable to battle!"

The announcer then reminded everyone of the tally. It was the second win of the match for Leon, making it four against four.

"Excellent work, Dragapult!" Leon praised his Pokémon.

On the other side of the arena, Ash was also full of

admiration for his Pokémon. "Lucario, return," he said. "You gave it all you had." Ash meant what he said. He believed in his Pokémon. But this was a tough battle. "I already knew Leon's strong! Even if I'm ahead, he catches up!" Could he remember that he believed in himself, too?

"Leon looks like he's not even trying," Sonia said from her seat in the bleachers, her voice heavy with concern for Ash.

"Oh, Ash," Chloe said with a worried sigh. Chloe knew how much Ash and Lucario had been through. She knew it must have been hard for Ash to lose Lucario so early in the battle, especially when it was due to the Dragon-Tail switch, not Ash's choice.

"He'll be fine," Dawn assured her. "No need to worry!"

Team Rocket was worried, too. "Dragapult's just too powerful." James moaned.

"This could be bad news for the twerp," Meowth agreed.

"Get it together!" Jessie demanded, yelling down at the arena floor. "We're up here cheering our little lungs out!"

Back on the field, Leon asked, "What now, Ash? My Dragapult can still go the distance."

"Dragapult," Dragapult purred confidently.

Ash narrowed his eyes and grabbed a Poké Ball. "Dragonite, I choose you!"

This time, Dragonite looked locked in and determined.

"Use Hurricane, let's go!" Ash demanded.

Dragonite began to flap its wings with conviction, and a rush of air swept through the arena.

"Those gale-force winds are bombarding Dragapult!" the announcer said. Dragapult could not move in a straight line! The wind tossed it to and fro.

"Awesome! It's working," Ash cheered.

In the stands, the crowd felt the power of the Hurricane move. Their hair whipped around, and tears streamed from their eyes.

Leon directed Dragapult, "Let loose a huge Thunderbolt!" The electric energy crackled all around, then the air stilled.

"Did that Thunderbolt just neutralize the Hurricane?" the announcer asked, shocked.

A lone streak of lightning zapped Dragonite.

"Well, well. Is that the best you can do?" Leon asked, hands on his hips.

"In that case . . . Fly high, Dragonite!" Ash pumped his fist in the air.

"Use Dragon Darts!" Leon called, knowing that the

move ranked as one of Dragapult's best. Dragapult shot off the Dreepy darts. One! Two!

With Dragonite high above the stadium floor, Ash called, "Draco Meteor, go!" He watched to see how his plan would unfold. Dragonite sent a gleaming hot-pink meteor into the sky. It exploded like a firework!

"Now, Dragapult, dodge them all!" Leon directed. Dragapult soared up, dodging the meteors. The Dreepy darts couldn't swerve fast enough, and they were shot down. One! Two! But Dragapult kept zipping upward, closing in on Dragonite.

"Dragonite, quick! Grab on to Dragapult!" Ash advised, and Dragonite dove toward its opponent.

"Use Thunderbolt!" Leon called, trying to stop whatever Ash had planned before it got started.

Dragapult was sizzling with energy, but Dragonite latched on, wrapping its front legs around the other Pokémon. The two plunged toward the stadium floor, the power of the Thunderbolt move zapping all around them. They were in a spinning free fall!

"All right, use Dragonite Meteor!" Ash yelled.

"*Dragonite* Meteor?" Leon sounded uncertain.

Sonia and Hop were also in shock. "So now Dragonite's the meteor?!" Hop gasped.

Chloe's face was all concern while Dawn couldn't help but feel the rush. She pumped her arms into the air and yelled, "Go, go, go!"

Dragonite and Dragapult slammed into the ground with a thud that shook the stadium to the top row of seats. A thick cloud of dust rose around the Pokémon . . . When it cleared, Dan moved in to make a call.

"Dragapult is unable to battle!" he announced. Dragonite slowly lifted itself from the ground.

Dragon Tail had given Ash more than he had bargained for, and Dragonite had to work hard to make sure they wouldn't have to deal with that momentum-changing move again. But now Ash had won his third matchup of the battle!

"Pika." Pikachu sighed with relief.

Ash took off his hat and wiped his forehead. "Thanks a lot, Dragonite," he said.

Dragonite looked back at Ash and Pikachu and shared a smile.

Leon called Dragapult back to its Poké Ball. "You were amazing!" he said to it. Then he looked across the arena to his challenger. "Ash, you are the absolute best!" he called.

Ash looked surprised to get such an outright compliment from Leon at this stage of the competition.

"But wait. Have you noticed?" Leon continued. "Take a look at your Pokémon. They already appear quite exhausted." Leon was reminding Ash why he, the Monarch, still had the upper hand. Leon's Pokémon were fresh! Ash might be leading with four remaining Pokémon to Leon's three, but Ash's team had all already taken damage.

"Pika?" Pikachu gave Ash an uncertain look.

"Rillaboom, let's go!" Leon commanded, and his next Pokémon appeared.

CHAPTER NINE

Rillaboom stood at its full height, on its two feet, and lifted its gigantic fists in the air. *"Riiiiiil!"* it roared. With its head of thick, green, leaflike hair, Leon's Pokémon looked as if it came straight from the jungle.

It pulled a drum from the strap on its back and slapped it down on the ground. Two wooden drumsticks appeared from Rillaboom's green cuffs. The Drummer Pokémon twirled the drumsticks and began to pound its drum. *Boom, boom, boom.* It sent vibrations through everything and everyone in the stadium.

In such a back-and-forth match, it was a challenge for either Trainer to maintain momentum, and Dragonite seemed troubled after Rillaboom's bold entrance onto the battlefield.

Boom, tap, boom, tap, boom, tap! Boom, boom, boom, boom!

"Dragonite, take extra care!" Ash advised. He gritted his teeth.

"You can do it, Dragonite!" Dawn cheered.

"Give it your all, Ash!" Chloe added.

Leon kept things moving. "Drum Beating, go!" Rillaboom spun its drumsticks again and then went back to pounding. With each strike of the drum, bark-covered roots sprang forth, forging a path toward Dragonite.

"Hurricane!" Ash countered. He watched the Drum Beating intensify as it grew closer to Dragonite. The roots were as thick as tree trunks, and they grew like

weeds. They bounded into the air and reached for Dragonite as the Hurricane winds blew.

"Dragonite just let loose with a powerful Hurricane!" the announcer said. *"It's a Flying-type move, which is super effective against Grass-type Rillaboom!"*

Rillaboom let out a stupendous roar and began pounding even faster.

"That Drum Beating move is surprisingly strong, lessening the damage from Hurricane!" The announcer didn't need to tell the folks in the stadium. They could all see it for themselves!

Hop cheered for his brother from the stands. "Great stuff!"

Sonia was surprised at Rillaboom's power, and so was Team Rocket. Dragonite's Hurricane wind had become more of a gentle breeze.

"Let's go!" yelled Leon, and Rillaboom continued drumming. The twisting roots responded to Rillaboom's force and lashed out, slashing at Dragonite, attacking it in the air. They made contact again and again until Dragonite fell to the ground.

"Dragonite, are you all right?" Ash asked. Dragonite wobbled to its feet.

In the skybox, Diantha pointed out that Dragonite now had lowered speed. "It's an effect of the Drum Beating." Cynthia nodded. The two accomplished Trainers really could witness everything that happened on the battlefield, and they understood the effects of the various moves. They could see the momentum start to shift from one Trainer to the other.

"When I bring out my Grass type, a lot of opponents tend to use Flying-type attacks," Leon said. "This is how we counter that."

Dawn shook her head. "Offense is the greatest defense? Seems like Leon is acting a bit like Ash does," she realized. "Don't you think that both of them have similar battling styles?" Dawn wondered to Chloe.

One thing was clear: both Trainers were giving it all they had.

"Bring it even more, Ash!" Leon called.

"Use Dragonite Meteor!" Ash yelled. It was the attack that had brought down Dragapult!

Dragonite dove through the air, flanked by a squad of bright pink meteors.

"Rillaboom, use Drum Beating." Leon advised his Pokémon to stick with the same move. It was working so far!

"Break through it, now!" Ash shouted, but before Dragonite could reach Rillaboom, a woody root wrapped itself around Dragonite's belly and took hold.

"Oh no!" Ash cried out.

"Too bad, Ash. I anticipated that move," Leon admitted.

Dragonite whimpered as the root lifted it high in the air, tightening its grip.

"That looks similar to Vine Whip," Professor Oak observed from the viewing party back in the Kanto region.

"Bulbasaur," agreed Bulbasaur, one of Ash's most loyal Pokémon. Vine Whip was Bulbasaur's

move. Now it watched Ash along with the rest of his Pokémon.

The root waved Dragonite around like a flag and then whacked it against the dusty stadium floor. The only good news was that Dragonite managed to break loose! It did a backward flip and landed on its feet. Dragonite was not happy. It was furious! It took off, aiming at Rillaboom at full speed.

"Let's finish this! Use Dragon Claw!" Ash directed, and Dragonite's paws glowed a neon green.

"Acrobatics!" Leon countered. Leon's call made it easy for Rillaboom to bound away from all Dragonite's punches.

"Speedy!" James noted.

"That lug's light on its legs," Meowth agreed.

Dragonite stuck with Dragon Claw, swiping at Rillaboom with all its might. First one paw, then the other—but neither ever made contact. Rillaboom leaped right over Dragonite's head. And then, after Dragonite missed another punch, Rillaboom caught it off-balance. Rillaboom landed one good hit, and then another, and Dragonite was down for the count.

"Dragonite!" Ash yelled.

Dan hovered above Ash's Dragon type. Dragonite

let out a little moan. “Dragonite is unable to battle,” the referee confirmed.

Rillaboom continued to bang its drum as if celebrating its triumph.

“Rillaboom didn’t even waver in spite of the type disadvantage! Great high-level battling!” the announcer exclaimed.

“That’s my bro,” Hop said with pride.

Now Ash and Leon each had three Pokémon left.

Ash called Dragonite in to take a rest. “You did awesome,” he told it proudly. They had come so far together. Next, he had to move on to another battling companion. “’Kay, Sirfetch’d, I choose you!” he declared.

"Sirfetch'd!" Ash's Fighting type appeared on the battlefield, leek and shield clasped in its wings.

"Meteor Assault," Ash yelled fresh out of the gate. At once, the energy began to build all around Sirfetch'd, radiating an intense yellow.

"High Horsepower!" Leon called on a new move. Rillaboom put away its drumsticks, then began to run, thundering toward Sirfetch'd.

Sirfetch'd, a gleaming force, surged toward Rillaboom.

"A head-on collision!" the announcer cried as the two Pokémon met in the center. *"Can they compete in terms of power?!"*

They appeared equally matched. They were both

pushing with all their might. Rillaboom was holding its ground, but Sirfetch'd was dealing a lot of damage with the sheer force of its assault. There was a lot of grunting!

"Hang in there," Leon yelled.

"Let's go!" Ash yelled.

Sirfetch'd gave one last shove and sent Rillaboom barreling backward until it smacked into its own drum.

Sirfetch'd was left panting. Meteor Assault was its signature move, but it was draining. *"Sirfetch'd,"* it grumbled with satisfaction.

"Awesome!" cheered Ash.

Dan came down on his hovercraft and loomed over where Rillaboom sat motionless . . . but then the Drummer Pokémon reached a mighty hand out and placed it on its drum. It was unsteady, but it forced itself to standing.

Even though Rillaboom could barely stay upright after the hit, Sirfetch'd couldn't take advantage of it. That was the high cost of Meteor Assault—Sirfetch'd needed time to build up its energy again.

CHAPTER TEN

Poor Sirfetch'd! The Meteor Assault attack had been legendary, but it was not easy to bounce back from a head-on collision. The Fighting type needed time!

Leon called out, "High Horsepower!" And just like that, Rillaboom was on the offensive again, and its hit sent Sirfetch'd tumbling through the air.

Ash assessed the battlefield. "Quick! Jump on your shield, Sirfetch'd!" he directed.

"Drum Beating!" Leon declared.

Rillaboom returned to the damage-dealing Grass-type move, and the pesky roots sprang from the ground.

Sirfetch'd flipped through the air, landed on its shield, and then surfed on it along the roots toward

Rillaboom. *"Sir-fetch'd, sir-fetch'd,"* the Wild Duck Pokémon grunted.

"Fury Cutter, quick!" Ash called.

"Acrobatics!" Leon countered.

Sirfetch'd rose up and readied its leek for a diving attack. Then it zoomed down at full force.

A white glow illuminated Rillaboom. It first dodged Sirfetch'd's strikes, and then scored a direct hit, and another. Sirfetch'd spun out of control and skidded to a stop on the stadium floor.

Sirfetch'd lay sprawled on the ground. It held out its leek, trying to prop itself up. But it was only able to lift its noble beak.

"Sirfetch'd is unable to battle!" Dan confirmed.

Hop cheered. "That's what Lee is all about!"

"Ash has now lost two Pokémon in a row," the announcer informed the crowd, *"while Leon and Rillaboom have been able to control the airspace in this fierce battle!"*

"Sirfetch'd, return now!" Ash said, holding out a Poké Ball. "Thanks for taking us this far."

On the other end of the arena, Leon wanted Rillaboom to know he had no plans to switch it out. "You're doing just what you need to do!" Leon called to Rillaboom, who responded with a quick nod and roar.

Jessie and James pouted and whined about Leon's lead.

Meowth had more faith. "Nope! Pikachu and Dracovish are still in this thing!"

Leon called out, "Ash, thanks to you and your Pokémon, *my* Pokémon and I are truly living up to our greatest potential!"

Ash clenched his fists.

Leon continued, "But it's really kind of sad. You have two Pokémon. True, this battle has been great, but it's soon about to end." Was Leon getting a little too sure of himself?

"No battle is over until it's over!" Ash reminded the reigning Champion. "Now, Dracovish, I choose you!"

"Dra-co-vish," Ash's Pokémon said as it flipped and landed facing Leon and Rillaboom. Then Dracovish roared. It was back and ready to battle.

"Wow, Dracovish is continuing on its spiky path!" the announcer pointed out, reminding everyone of the curious transformation that had started when Dracovish had matched up against Dragapult. Dracovish's spikes were still glowing with their new mystery power.

"Ice Fang, let's go!" Ash called. Dracovish began to run at Rillaboom, its fangs glowing an icy blue as it exhaled clouds of frosty breath.

"Use Drum Beating!" Leon demanded.

Rillaboom raised its arms and twirled its drumsticks, letting out a long roar. As soon as it began the pounding drumbeat, the move's thick, imposing roots started to arch across the arena floor. They grew directly in the path of Dracovish, who ran right into them and bounced off.

Dracovish threw itself at the roots again, but they didn't budge. So the Fossil Pokémon opened its gigantic mouth and clamped down on the roots. Its frigid fangs sent ice crystals straight into them.

"Look at that! It ripped Drum Beating to pieces!" the announcer said, amazed.

Rillaboom roared with frustration!

"Dracovish, use Dragon Rush!" Ash called, trying to take advantage of the momentum.

Leon countered with High Horsepower.

Dracovish pitched forward. As it ran, the aura of a mystical dragon surrounded it, building its power. And Dracovish, in honor of its teammate Sirfetch'd, put its all into the attack.

Rillaboom and Dracovish collided in the middle of the arena floor. The dragon aura pulsed with energy,

and a dragon head rose into the sky. At the end of the attack, Rillaboom collapsed.

Dan's hoverboard lowered toward the arena floor. "Rillaboom is unable to battle," he determined.

Dracovish let out a triumphant roar, its belly spikes still glowing.

"Yeah! We did it!" Ash yelled. His words were filled with relief.

"Ash caught up almost immediately," the announcer said, but everyone knew the Monarch still had two well-rested, healthy Pokémon left to battle.

"Rillaboom, return," Leon said, his tone upbeat. "I like the way you battled. Thanks!"

"Okay, Dracovish! Keep your guard up!" Ash warned.

"Draco."

Leon tossed a Poké Ball into the arena. "Cinderace, let's go!"

The Pokémon bounced on the balls of its feet, ready for its next matchup.

"There you are," Ash murmured. Because Goh had had a Cinderace partner for much of their journey together, Ash felt an odd connection to Leon's Cinderace, and its fur markings and competitive energy felt familiar. Still, Ash did not have a plan to defeat Leon's Striker Pokémon. He needed to come up with one, pronto!

"Use High Jump Kick!" Leon started things off.

"It's now a Fighting type," the announcer explained. Cinderace's special Ability let it change its own type to match the moves it used. *"And High Jump Kick is a direct hit!"*

Dracovish and Ash hadn't even had time for a counterattack!

"Use Water Gun!" Ash belted out, trying a Water-type move.

Leon countered with Pyro Ball. Cinderace spun and shot off a flaming sphere with incredible speed. It met

Dracovish's icy-blue move head-on—and the two powerful attacks canceled each other out.

"Fishious Rend!" Ash sounded desperate, already using this big move. Dracovish's jaw and stomach spikes began to gleam as it thundered across the arena. It bounded into the air for a diving attack.

"Use Iron Head," Leon countered quickly, and the tuft of fur between Cinderace's two ears turned metallic, glimmering with its new power. Cinderace rose into the air to meet Dracovish head-on.

The impact pushed the Fossil Pokémon back. Dracovish fell flat, but Cinderace landed gracefully on its two fur-padded feet.

"So now it's a Steel type?" Ash muttered with frustration.

"Very nice header, Ash!" Leon called out playfully.

"Leon's definitely setting the pace," Cynthia observed from the skybox. She could see how Ash was struggling. Even his posture had changed. His shoulders were thrown forward, his stance rigid. Ash was feeling the pressure.

"Dracovish, are you all right?" Ash called.

"Draco," Dracovish insisted. Then it scoffed at Cinderace.

"Cinder, Cinderace," the Striker Pokémon responded, not showing any wear or tear.

"Pika, pika!" Pikachu chimed in, cheering its teammate on.

"Let's finish this now! Use Dragon Rush!" Ash called.

Dracovish responded immediately, surging forward with incredible speed. A crystal-blue Dragon aura again surrounded the Fossil Pokémon as it raced toward Cinderace.

"Use High Jump Kick!" Leon yelled.

The fur at Cinderace's knees began to gleam, and Cinderace took off running. As it neared Dracovish, it lifted high into the air. Then Cinderace dove down,

pouncing on Dracovish. A cloud of dust rose up. When it settled, Cinderace was still standing, but Dracovish was not.

"Dracovish is unable to battle!" Dan said.

"And Cinderace claims victory over Dracovish!" the announcer confirmed.

Ash held out a Poké Ball for Dracovish to return. "You really did your best," he told his Pokémon.

"Do you think they'll be all right?" Chloe asked Dawn.

"They'll be fine," Dawn reassured her friend. "Those two can handle anything!"

CHAPTER ELEVEN

Ash and Pikachu's fans had so much faith in them! Meanwhile, Leon had a new battle strategy. "You battled well. Return!" he said to Cinderace. He then took out another Poké Ball. "Ash, this is my sixth Pokémon! Charizard, let's go!"

Charizard landed in a commanding pose. Its massive, steel-blue wings were spread wide, and its determined eyes smoldered. Add in its fangs, claws, and flaming tail, and Charizard was the very vision of power.

"Leon has called on his strongest partner, Charizard!" the announcer said. But anyone who was a fan of Leon or the World Coronation Series already knew Charizard, and they knew all about Leon's bond with his Flame Pokémon. These two had won it all the year before!

"So, he wants to finish the match using Charizard, huh?" Ash said. He looked to Pikachu. They raised a fist to each other.

"Pika!" Pikachu was ready.

"You're up, buddy!" Ash confirmed.

Pikachu galloped out onto the battlefield, stopping near the center. Standing on all fours, Pikachu looked tiny as it faced Charizard. But it also looked confident.

The announcer took the chance to remind everyone watching just how dire things were for Ash. *"Pikachu has become Ash's last hope! But can Ash and Pikachu stop Charizard? Or will Leon bring it to an end here and now?"*

Leon called to his opponent. "Charizard was my

very first Pokémon," he said. "It's gone on all my adventures. My partner from the very beginning. My very first battle. My very first catch. My very first Evolution. Time and time again, it's been there with me." Leon smiled at his memories.

"I hear you, Leon!" Ash replied. His voice was even, and his words were thoughtful. "I've gone on every adventure with Pikachu! That's why I want Pikachu to beat Charizard!"

"Pikaaaa!"

Leon scoffed, but he had to chuckle. He raised his hand and zapped Charizard back into its Poké Ball. "I hear *you*. So, I'm winning with Charizard!" Leon held the Poké Ball out to his side. The Poké Ball began to glow from within, and then it increased its size, again and again, looking like a glittering pink disco ball. Leon heaved the ball into the air and yelled, "Gigantamax!"

Charizard appeared in the middle of the stadium, its wings blazing with flames. It quadrupled in size in an instant, and then did it again. Its gigantic eyes were now yellow with deep red pupils. Magenta energy whirled around the massive Pokémon. Above the stadium, a dark, swirling cloud appeared.

“Wow, it’s huge!” Meowth observed.

“Someone’s going to get super squished,” James predicted.

Gigantamax Charizard growled, shaking the stadium. Its yellow belly radiated light and energy.

“Let’s go, Pikachu!” Ash yelled, undeterred. “Use Thunderbolt!”

“Pikaaaaa—” Electricity coursed through Pikachu.

“Now . . . Max Rockfall!” Leon called. Gigantamax Charizard generated an enormous boulder that slowly crashed toward Pikachu.

“Quick, get out of there!” warned Ash.

Pikachu shot up into the air, but not high enough to

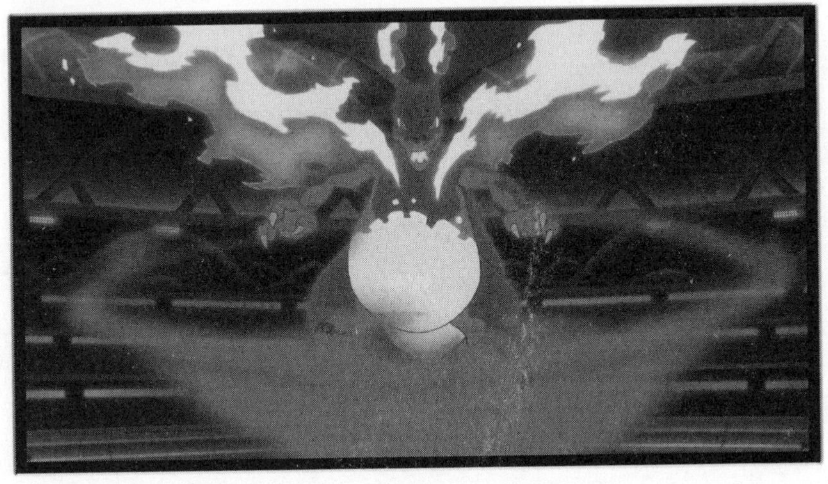

escape the effects of Max Rockfall. After the boulder hit the ground, it kicked up a sandstorm full of rocks that whirled around Pikachu.

"Pikachu is having more and more of its strength drained away as it soars above Charizard!" the announcer explained.

Pikachu was high in the stadium, at Gigantamax Charizard's eye level. "Iron Tail, let's go!" Ash called.

Pikachu's tail grew bright with energy as the Pokémon went in with one of its signature moves. Pikachu landed Iron Tail right between Charizard's eyes—but it had no effect at all.

Gigantamax Charizard growled as if it were

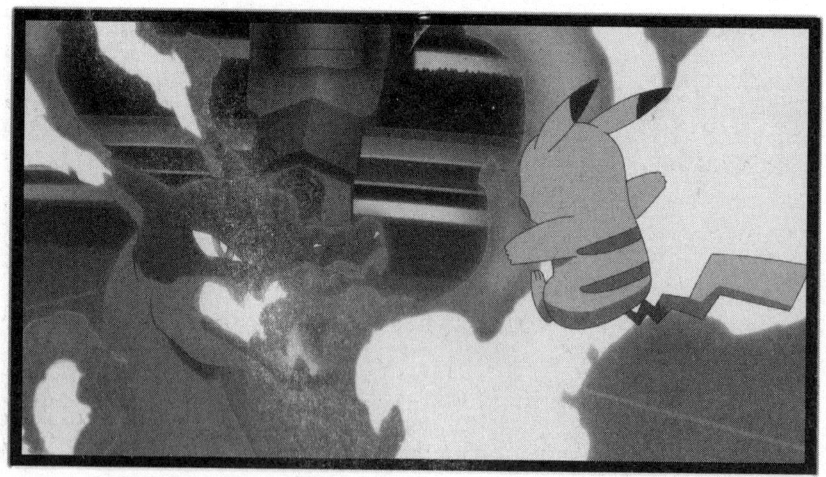

annoyed. Oversized flames escaped from the corners of its mouth.

Pikachu gasped. Its move had failed.

Ash couldn't help but murmur his partner's name with concern.

Leon continued to call the shots and set the pace. "Use Max Wyrmwind!" he directed.

Gigantamax Charizard unleashed a bright pink funnel cloud of power that swirled around Pikachu. The whole stadium seemed to hum with the force of the battle move.

"No, Pikachu!" Ash called in concern.

"It's over," Hop said confidently from his seat in the stands. He'd seen his brother commandeer a battle at this stage time and time again.

But Hop had never seen his brother battle *Ash* in an official battle. There was a first time for everything.

CHAPTER TWELVE

When the Wyrmwind lifted, Pikachu was panting but still standing.

"Nice endurance," Leon said with a smile.

Ash smiled back. "Gigantamaxing is so cool!" he blurted. "Awesome power . . ." He loved using his Gigantamax boost with Gengar, but he and Pikachu shared a special move, too. Ash looked down at his arm where his yellow-and-black Z-Ring was wrapped around his wrist. "We'll have to use this."

"Pika-pi!" Pikachu called to Ash, telling him that it was a go. The partners were ready; they shared a plan.

Ash tossed his baseball cap to Pikachu to start their transformation ritual. *"Pika!"* Pikachu gave a happy chirp as it pulled the hat on.

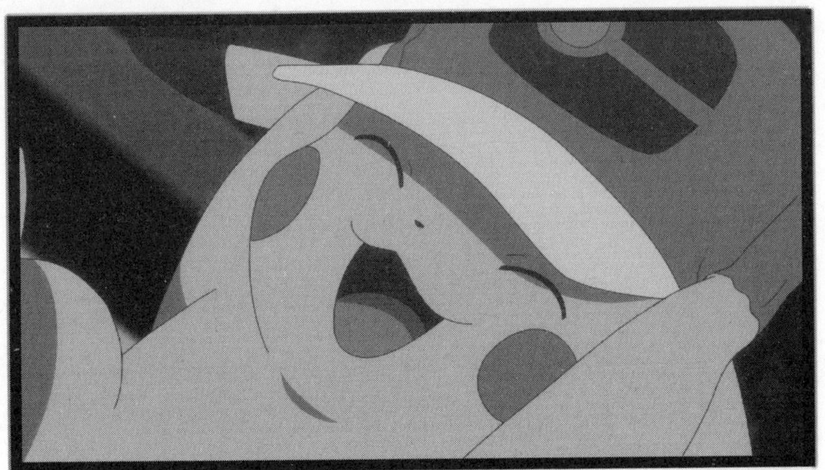

"Yeah, we're going all-out!" Ash cried. He and Pikachu bumped fists, excited. The team was in sync!

"I've been waiting for this!" Leon admitted.

"Here we go!" the announcer revved up the crowd. *"Ash and Pikachu have begun their Z-Move!"*

The partners moved in sync, striking the poses to prepare the move. Electricity streamed between them. "Much bigger than a Thunderbolt . . ." Ash declared. "Pikachu, use ten-million-volt Thunderbolt!"

"Pika, pika, pika, pika, pika, pikaaaaaa!" Brilliant rays of energy in all colors coursed from Pikachu as the power of the Z-Move took hold. It burst into rainbow meteors that streamed across the arena toward Gigantamax Charizard.

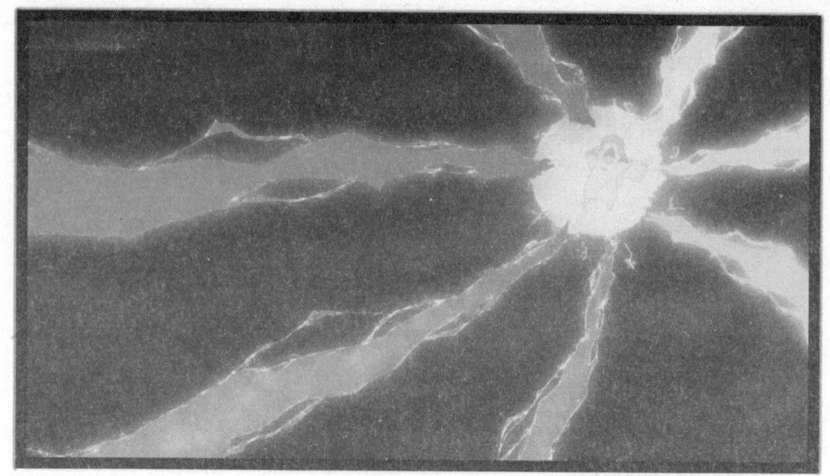

"Let's have a champion time!" Leon exclaimed. "Use G-Max Wildfire!" Gigantamax Charizard sent dragon-shaped flames flying straight at the pulses of Pikachu's Z-Move. The two moves met in the center of the stadium with an explosion that sent a huge beam of power into the sky. "This is it, Ash! What I've always wanted to see! Gigantamax versus a Z-Move!"

"Yeah, Leon. Me too!" Ash called back.

"This massive amount of energy is shaking Wyndon Stadium down to its very foundation!" the announcer cried. And he was not exaggerating! The arena floor was crumbling.

Pikachu and Gigantamax Charizard maintained their intensity. Pikachu grunted with exertion.

Gigantamax Charizard snarled. The collision of the two moves was building a huge sphere of energy that pulsed in the center of the stadium. The fans in the stands had to shield their eyes from the light, and the swirling winds forced them back against their seats. The beam of power sizzled and crackled against dark clouds in the sky.

In another part of the Galar Region, Professor Magnolia, the famous Pokémon researcher, was checking the numbers in her lab. Something was not right. "What is this Galar particle reaction?" she wondered. "I've never seen this during my observations."

She stood before the enormous high-tech cage keeping the Legendary Pokémon Eternatus locked up for safety.

The Gigantic Pokémon was agitated. Suddenly, it reared its skeletal head and bashed it against its prison! Eternatus roared, then blasted up into the sky, shattering its cage on the way.

The lab workers gasped and covered their heads as glass streamed down around them.

“Is it another Darkest Day?” Professor Magnolia worried. Was the Galar region once again in danger from the extremely powerful Eternatus?

CHAPTER THIRTEEN

Back at Wyndon Stadium, it wasn't long before the crowd began to realize that there was something in the air . . . literally. After a huge explosion, the brilliant beam of energy from the super battle moves dissolved into thousands of glowing pink particles. They floated under a massive, dark, swirling cloud in the sky that crackled with blue lightning.

"Hey, is that . . . ?" Hop asked, looking up.

Sonia also watched the cloud. "Yes," she answered, her voice full of dread. "With the collision of Gigantamax and Z-Move, and the enormous power of Mega Evolution . . ." She paused to think. She realized they were observing something entirely new. It was overwhelming . . . and daunting. "Is it affecting Wyndon Stadium and the space-time here?"

The announcer was also perplexed. *"What is going on here? Charizard's Gigantamax effect has worn off, but there is still a huge black cloud swirling above Wyndon Stadium!"*

It was true. Both Charizard and Pikachu had been returned to their original forms. After all the bursts of energy and cheers during battle, things were scarily silent inside the stadium. The black cloud swirled, the pink particles glowed, and the audience held its breath.

Then there was a roar.

"Pika."

Ash gasped, then mumbled, "That voice sounds like . . ."

He studied the sky above the stadium. Did he really hear what he thought he'd heard? Pikachu and Charizard were also transfixed by the churning skies.

Then he saw it. "Eternatus," Ash said. From far below, Ash could see its red glow.

"What's going on?" Leon wondered.

That's when everyone saw the huge, skeletal Pokémon circling in the dark skies. The audience let out a collective gasp. Eternatus roared again.

"Could that actually be . . ." the Wyndon announcer

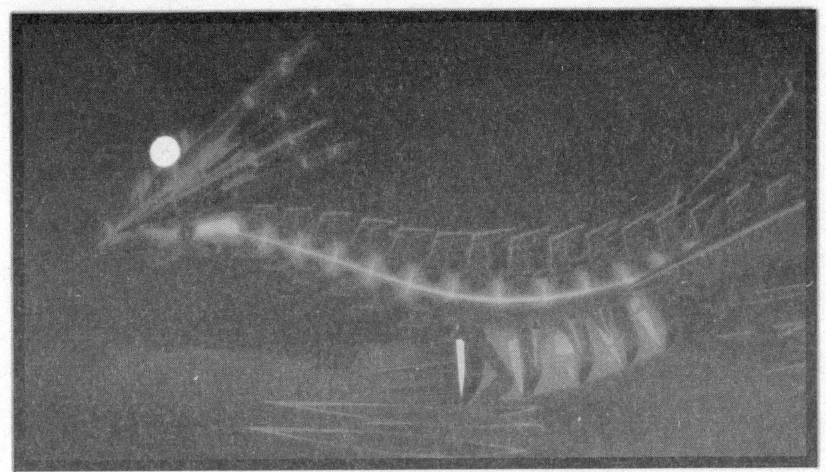

began. He then paused, trying to understand what he was seeing. *"Could that be the Pokémon who threw the entire Galar region into chaos—Eternatus?!"*

Eternatus roared again, but it did not seem angry. Its motions were smooth as it swiveled and circled above the stadium.

In the stands, Sonia could feel that roar vibrate in her bones. She knew the Pokémon that was circling overhead, and she worried what that meant. She quickly picked up her phone and called her grandmother—Professor Magnolia. "Gran, are things all right there? Eternatus appeared above Wyndon Stadium!"

"Yes, Sonia, we're fine," her grandmother assured her, looking around the lab. "Tell me, how are you?"

"The Galar particles above us are acting strangely!" Sonia said, watching the glowing pink particles below the ominous, swirling cloud.

"I see. Then it's possible Eternatus is reacting to that," Professor Magnolia considered.

She and Sonia, along with Leon, Ash, and Goh, had significant history with the Pokémon that was flying over the stadium like a humongous, ancient buzzard. Professor Magnolia and Sonia had spent years researching the Darkest Day, a storm of dark energy that took place long, long ago, related to Eternatus and the particle energy of Galar that made Dynamax and Gigantamax power-ups possible. It ended when the Pokémon was defeated. But last year, the scheming Chairman Rose brought Eternatus back. He wanted to use it as a source of energy, even though it caused Pokémon all over Galar to rampage out of control.

Leon, Ash, and Goh had combined their efforts against Eternatus in order to defeat Chairman Rose's devious plan, and it was Goh who finally captured Eternatus. Professor Magnolia then locked away Eternatus's Poké Ball, so they could prevent another Darkest Day, another disaster.

But then, the day before the World Coronation Series final match, Leon, Sonia, and Professor Magnolia told Ash and Goh about a new plan. Professor Magnolia had retrieved Eternatus and let it out of its Poké Ball.

"The thing is, staying asleep all the time isn't much of a life," Sonia had said.

"Eternatus has a deep connection to Galar particles, the energy that flows through this region," Professor Magnolia explained. "This is a Pokémon that cannot be separated from the Galarian way of life. We all must learn to coexist with Eternatus."

"The first step is to help it get used to people," Sonia said. "With a little help from Leon, of course."

Leon was slowly helping Eternatus adapt to a new life—one where Eternatus was able to control its power. While Leon was busy with the World Coronation Series finals, Professor Magnolia had taken Eternatus back to her lab, where they had all agreed the Gigantic Pokémon would be safe.

But now, Eternatus had broken out of the lab. The Pokémon glided through the black clouds in the sky—clouds that were a result of supernatural energy.

Suddenly, Eternatus stopped circling. It reared its head back and roared. Its core started glowing bright pink, crackling with sheer power, and it shot a Dynamax Cannon straight upward. The magenta-colored beam of energy, full of Galar particles, seemed to rip a hole in the black clouds. The darkness above the stadium dissolved, revealing a sky of brilliant blue.

The move also caused a huge rush of wind—which lifted Pikachu off the ground! Ash ran forward and held on tight to his partner while Charizard and Leon braced themselves against the gusts.

Then, in an instant, the air was calm. The glimmering pink particles, as light as dandelion puffs,

drifted down into the arena. And Eternatus was still there, circling over them.

Sonia was trying to figure out what had just happened. "Eternatus . . . But why?" she asked her grandmother.

"The stability of Galar particles *is* the stability of the Galar region," Professor Magnolia said. The Gigantamax and Z-Move combined must have caused Galar-particle activity that was too intense. Eternatus had stabilized them. "Eternatus appears to have just protected every one of us. And the region's peace."

Eternatus let out a soft roar, almost like a purr, then flew up and away.

"Pika," Pikachu said, watching the ancient Pokémon disappear from view.

"Eternatus, thanks so much," Leon called into the air.

Next to Sonia, Hop was in awe. "How cool was that?"

"I hope it will keep watching over us in the future," Sonia mused, the pink particles still drifting in the air.

Team Rocket was also amazed. "To protect the world from devastation," Jessie began the old Team Rocket rhyme.

"To defend all people within our nation," James added.

"To illuminate with beams of truth and of love," said Jessie, improvising.

"To extend its reach to the stars above," followed James.

"Rocking Eternatus love," Meowth concluded.

"Wobbuffet."

Never had truer words been spoken by Team Rocket.

CHAPTER FOURTEEN

"Now, I think it's time we got back to the match," the announcer said, trying to focus everyone back on the battle.

Leon realized Eternatus had left them one more parting gift. "Amazing! Eternatus gave us a bonus round!" He held his illuminated wristband in the air.

Ash realized his Dynamax band was powered up again as well.

"Pika," Pikachu murmured, seeing the light shining from Ash's band. Ash and Leon both had another chance to Gigantamax! Gigantamaxing twice in one match was unprecedented!

"I hope you're watching, Eternatus!" Leon yelled, holding out a Poké Ball. "Charizard, return! Cinderace, I'm going with you!"

Leon's Poké Ball began to glimmer and glow, doubling in size until it barely fit in Leon's palm. As he threw it to the center of the arena, Leon yelled, "Gigantamax!" The call created all the blazing energy that it usually did, utilizing the power of Galar particles. Soon, an imposing Gigantamax Cinderace stood on top of an enormous burning ball that had a face of flames.

Ash, holding Pikachu in one arm, took it all in. Gigantamax Cinderace was quite a spectacle! "Pikachu, buddy," Ash said, "what do you say we go for it?"

"Pikachu!"

Pikachu's willing response made Ash laugh! "All right, then. Let's go big!" Ash said. He grasped Pikachu in both hands and hurled his partner into the air. "Gigantamax!" he yelled.

A pink aura of energy surrounded the Mouse Pokémon as it flew upward. Then a mighty pink bolt zapped Pikachu. *"Pi, pi, pi,"* Pikachu said each time it increased in size. By the time it landed on the stadium floor, Gigantamax Pikachu was even taller than Gigantamax Cinderace on its ball of flames. Gigantamax Pikachu still had its sly smile, but its lightning-bolt tail was longer and glowed with an intense white light. Now, compared to Gigantamax Pikachu, Ash looked smaller than a tiny Mouse Pokémon!

"Oh, woooooow!" Chloe and Dawn were shocked by Pikachu's size.

The announcer could not contain his excitement. *"What a revolutionary climax of the Masters Eight Tournament Finals!"* Purple clouds above the stadium churned with Gigantamax energy.

Leon kept things moving. "Now, let's wrap this up, Cinderace! Use G-Max Fireball!"

Gigantamax Cinderace leaped to the ground and

proceeded to heave the massive fireball into the sky with a full-strength kick. Then it soared up after the ball, using its supersized ears as wings.

“No way we'll lose, Pikachu!” Ash assured his longtime partner. “Use G-Max Volt Crash!”

Pikachu jumped up and stomped on the stadium floor, rattling the bleachers to the top row. Electric energy surged from its red cheeks. Then it dropped to all fours and shot a single high-volt charge into the clouds.

Just as Pikachu finished its move, Gigantamax Cinderace sent the burning ball zooming toward the Pokémon. Pikachu pushed back against the Fireball with its tremendous arms, trying to hold it off. Then

Cinderace was caught off guard by the return of the G-Max Volt Crash as it surged back down into the stadium. Cinderace kicked its powerful legs against the Volt Crash, spinning it and trying to avoid getting blasted.

But the electric force kept pushing Cinderace down . . . and while Pikachu still pushed against the Fireball, its arms were losing strength, and it started to be pushed back by the Fireball's awesome power.

"Both Pokémon seem to be enduring it!" the announcer said. Then, there were two simultaneous explosions, and two clouds of smoke where the Gigantamax Pokémon had been. *"And they're both direct hits!"*

As the smoke lifted, so did the dark, swirling cloud above.

Ash could see Pikachu, small again, panting but standing on its hind feet.

"You all right?" Ash asked.

On the other side of the stadium, Cinderace was also back to its normal size. It was hunched over, appearing off-balance.

"Cinderace!" Leon called, checking on his Pokémon.

"Both Pokémon exerted so much power that they returned to their normal sizes!" said the announcer. Both Pokémon had only managed one G-Max move!

Cinderace looked over at Pikachu and started to smile, but then staggered and fell down.

Dan's hoverboard buzzed in at once. "Cinderace is unable to battle!" he announced.

CHAPTER FIFTEEN

"The face-off between Gigantamax Pokémon ends with a victory for Pikachu!" the announcer confirmed. Now Leon and Ash each had only one Pokémon remaining.

"Yes! Great, Pikachu!" Ash cheered.

"Pikaaa!" Pikachu declared. They were both pumped up, ready for one last battle!

Eevee, Piplup, and their Trainers celebrated in the stands. Pom-poms were shaking! And Team Rocket attempted gleeful leg kicks as they cheered, "Pi-ka-chu! Pi-ka-chu!"

Of course, Hop was worried for his big brother, the Monarch, who had been undefeated all season. Sonia wanted both Trainers to feel good about their showing. And Diantha and Cynthia were relishing the fact that it had become a real competition, with Ash keeping pace!

"Cinderace, return! You were the best," Leon said, his voice full of gratitude. "Great job Gigantamaxing." Then Leon turned to his worthy opponent. "All right, Ash! This will decide it! It's time to use our aces!"

"Yeah! Partner versus partner!" Ash called out. Pikachu made double fists, feeling fierce.

"Charizard, let's go!" Leon called as he threw his last Poké Ball.

Charizard exploded onto the stadium floor, wings wide and mouth open in a roar.

It had all come down to the two Pokémon that each Trainer had known the longest—the Pokémon who knew them best.

On the sidelines, Ash was stretching his arms, bending his legs, keeping limber.

"You did very well to drive someone like me this far!" Leon complimented his young challenger. "You're helping me become stronger than ever! So, until the last move, I say we get even more fired up!"

Charizard's tail blazed, and it reached out its neck and roared again, with feeling.

Pikachu dropped to all fours, electricity sizzling from its cheeks.

Ash replied, "Thanks to you, we've gotten a whole lot stronger than we were before, Leon. This battle is the peak of all the adventures Pikachu and I have had up to this point! That's why . . ." Ash paused for a moment and took a strong stance before proclaiming, "We're gonna win!"

Leon seemed shocked at Ash's confidence at first, but then he chuckled. The two Trainers truly were well matched.

"All right, Quick Attack!" Ash called.

"Use Ancient Power!" Leon directed Charizard.

Pikachu took off before Charizard's Rock-type move could get in its way.

"Pi-pi-pi, pi-pi-pi, pi-pi-pi!" Pikachu charged ahead, panting as it raced. It leaped over the rolling boulders from Charizard, using one as a springboard to pounce on Charizard's belly.

"And Pikachu's attack lands first!" narrated the announcer.

Charizard growled.

"Use Iron Tail!" directed Ash as Pikachu catapulted in the air.

"Pika, pika!"

“Knock it away!” Leon yelled as Pikachu came down, tail aglow.

Just as Pikachu was about to make contact, Charizard whacked the Mouse Pokémon with its flaming tail.

Pikachu skidded across the ground but landed on its feet.

“Use Air Slash!” belted Leon. The move pelted the ground all around Pikachu as it braced itself. There was nowhere to hide! Leon called for another move. “Use Fire Blast!”

“Electroweb!” Ash called. “Run, Pikachu!” His Pokémon managed to stop Charizard’s ball of fire for long enough to run out of the way.

“Thunderbolt, go!” Ash cried.

“Fire Blast, go!” Leon countered.

The two moves blasted each other, sending both Pokémon back.

“You all right?” Ash checked in with Pikachu. It had been a constant barrage!

“Can you still go on?” Leon asked Charizard, who grunted assent.

The crowd looked on with concern for both competitors.

"Use Iron Tail!" Ash called for one of their most effective moves.

"Charizard, take the hit!" Leon advised the Flame Pokémon. Charizard puffed up its chest. When Pikachu came zooming in and unleashed Iron Tail, Charizard did not flinch! It simply snarled as Pikachu landed the attack.

Immediately, Leon yelled, "Dragon Pulse!"

Pikachu could not retreat fast enough! Dragon Pulse came like a multicolored laser from deep in Charizard's throat. It encircled Pikachu and shot the Mouse Pokémon across the arena. Pikachu fought against it, grunting, but the final pulse left Pikachu

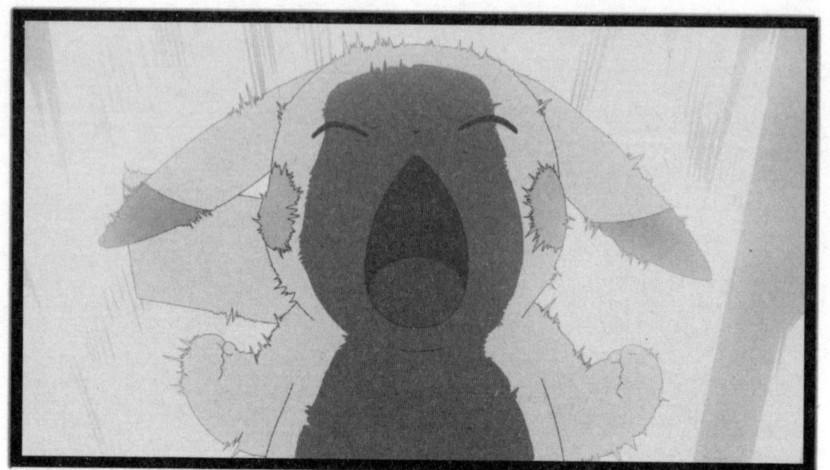

smoldering on the ground. Still, Pikachu pulled itself up onto its hind legs.

"We're not done!" Ash reassured his partner. "This is where it starts!" Ash's confidence energized Pikachu.

"Pikaaaaa!" Electricity danced all around Pikachu, proving it had plenty of fight left.

"I've gotta say, the two of you are the best!" Leon loved Ash's fighting spirit. "All right, then, Charizard, let's ramp it up!"

With that, Charizard roared and slapped its tail on the ground, fanning a host of flames to rival Pikachu's electric display.

"Go, Lee! Win this!" Hop cheered from above. "Beat them, *now*!"

Next to Hop, Sonia looked down at the Monarch. Seeing him so invested in a battle reminded her of what Leon had been like as a kid, when he first fell in love with Pokémon and battling.

"Pikachu, use Quick Attack!" Ash called.

In an instant, an unseen force knocked Charizard back. Quick Attack was fast!

"What was that?!" Hop asked. "I didn't see it!"

"Now! Ancient Power!" Leon demanded.

Charizard amped up the move, and a battalion of rocks targeted Pikachu. Pikachu began to hop onto the rocks, bounding from one to another as they rose into the air. Pikachu jumped higher and higher—until it was able to leap onto the huge metal archway that stretched across the top of the stadium! It galloped upside down along the arch at full force.

"Pika, pika, pika," Pikachu panted.

Charizard took flight, closing in on Pikachu. "Use Air Slash!" Leon cried. Charizard's blades of air slashed at Pikachu again and again. Pikachu flinched and dodged, barely escaping the move.

"Now, use Iron Tail!" Ash yelled from far below.

Up in the stands, Chloe gasped.

"Oh, wow," Dawn said in awe.

Pikachu was free-falling down from the arch, swiping at each hit of Air Slash with its own Iron Tail move as it fell. *"Pika, pika, pika,"* it grunted with each duck and dive. Then, it swerved in for a hit on Charizard, making direct contact across its head! But the hit didn't have much impact. Pikachu went spiraling to the hard ground, and Charizard came up ready to strike.

"Fire Blast!" Leon called. It was the strongest of all the Fire-type moves, and Charizard sent a red-hot firestorm right where Pikachu had landed.

"Thunderbolt!" Ash cried, but it was too late for

Pikachu to prepare the move. The ring of fire was already on top of the Mouse Pokémon.

Ash could only see smoke. The black cloud slowly lifted. *"Pikachu!"*

CHAPTER SIXTEEN

Leon and Charizard observed their opponents. Pikachu was on all fours, panting. Wisps of smoke rose from its body. It did not turn its head when Ash called. It just kept breathing. Everyone watching the battle was silent, waiting. Pikachu could see Dan on his hovercraft, slowly lowering into view.

Then Pikachu gulped, its cheeks sizzling, and fell over with a thud.

At first, everything was black for Pikachu. Only black. Pikachu felt confused. Then it heard a voice. A young voice. The voice of young Ash. “It’s so cute! It’s the best of all!” young Ash exclaimed. “Oh, hi, Pikachu!” Pikachu couldn’t see the young Ash, only hear him. But Pikachu remembered that Ash had said those words when they first met.

And then there was a shocking jolt of electricity, and Pikachu could see. At first, everything was white. Then Pikachu saw Bulbasaur, Squirtle, and Charizard, all staring down at it. Friends! So many friends, all around! Butterfree, Pidgeot, Primeape, Mr. Mime, Kingler, Snorlax, Tauros, Leavanny, Snivy, Oshawott, Greninja, Goodra. And so many more friends, from so many regions, many of whom Pikachu had not seen in such a long time. But where were they? Everything else besides the Pokémon was bright white.

Pikachu was still lying down. And then when Pikachu looked around, it was surrounded by even more familiar faces. Dragonite, Gengar, Lucario,

Sirfetch'd, and Dracovish. They were all so encouraging. And then Ash walked up and knelt down. Pikachu's partner. It was good to see Ash.

"You see, Pikachu? *Everybody's* backing us up!" Ash said. He made two fists and smiled.

Pikachu smiled. It felt at peace, hearing this. It was time.

"Pika . . ." Pikachu pulled its legs underneath it and forced itself to stand. The electricity zapped in its cheeks, then surged through its whole body! Suddenly, Pikachu snapped out of that other realm and was back in the stadium . . . blasting electricity to the sky, ready to go.

Leon gasped with surprise. Just like that, just as Dan was ready to make the call, Pikachu was back . . . and fully charged! A fresh surge of energy crackled around Pikachu, and it let off a wave of heat that swept through the whole stadium.

"Awesome, Pikachu! Way to go!" Ash cheered. He felt that old desire to prove that they could be the very best, that they were stronger than ever.

Leon smiled. "And that's the essence of Pikachu and Ash!" he declared with admiration.

Ash took hold of the bill of his cap and flipped it

backward. “Pikachu! We’re gonna put everything we’ve got into this attack!”

“Pika, pika!” The energy was nearly exploding from the Electric type’s tiny yellow-and-black body.

Leon raised an arm into the air for his signature pose. “Charizard! Let’s have a champion time!”

Pikachu and Charizard were as determined as ever. The power was churning inside both Pokémon.

“Thunderbolt! Let’s go!” Ash cried.

“Fire Blast! Now!” Leon yelled.

“Let’s go!” Ash and Leon exclaimed at the same time.

Both Pokémon summoned the strength for their

most intense attack. Pikachu thundered toward the center of the stadium floor, the voltage radiating all around. Charizard rumbled forward, its neck stretched out, its whole body ablaze. The two Pokémon and their moves clashed in the center in a huge blast of light. The Trainers screamed with exertion, seeing Pikachu and Charizard hit each other head-on.

There was roaring—from the Pokémon, the Trainers, and the fans . . .

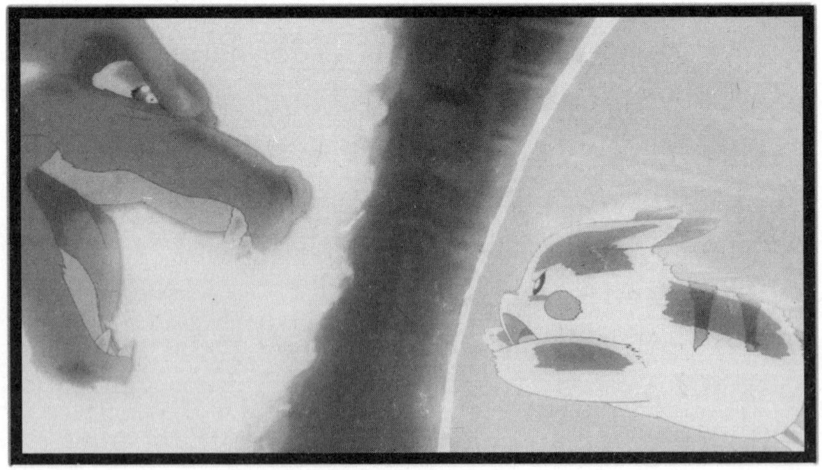

CHAPTER SEVENTEEN

"Hey, are you all right?" Ash asked with concern.

Pikachu felt confused again as it opened its eyes. But Ash was there. *"Pika-pi,"* Pikachu chirped in a small, sweet voice. *"Pikachu."*

They were in a Pokémon Center within the stadium, but Pikachu could not remember how they got there.

"Buddy, you were awesome. Incredible," Ash said. He grabbed on to one of Pikachu's paws with both hands. "That last attack of yours gave me the shivers!"

Pikachu slowly remembered all that had happened. It had been such an intense battle! Pikachu and Charizard had been in a full-force, head-on strike that had gone on and on. At last, it had ended. Pikachu had landed on all fours, exhausted. Charizard had wobbled on its hind legs, let out a mighty roar to the sky, and then . . . fallen backward.

Pikachu could hardly believe it was over. Dan had announced, "Charizard is unable to battle. Which means, the victory goes to . . . Ash!"

And then the announcer had declared, *"It's decided! We now have ourselves a new Champion! From the Kanto region, born in Pallet Town . . . Ash Ketchum!"*

"Pika-pi!" Pikachu had said with the last of its strength.

"Pikachu!" Ash had called. Just as Pikachu was about to collapse, Ash had run out to the center of the arena floor and lifted his Pokémon into his arms, laughing with joy.

Now, Pikachu jumped up on its bed, suddenly full of happy energy. *"Pika!"*

"Thanks *so* much," Ash said, looking over at Pikachu. "It's because of you that we were able to defeat Leon!" It had been their goal for so long!

"Pikachuuu!" It jumped into Ash's arms to hug him again. *"Pika, pika, pika!"*

Chloe, Dawn, Eevee, and Piplup watched from the observation window and shared their friends' joy.

Just then, a sliding door opened, and Leon and Charizard came in. "Looks like Pikachu is feeling better," Leon commented.

"Pika!"

"It was a good battle. Lots of fun, too!" Leon said.

"I feel the same exact way," Ash replied.

"It made me think back on my very first Pokémon battle," Leon said. "A great time! Yet frustrating . . ." Leon again could see flashes of that battle in his head, when he was young and Charizard was still a Charmander. They'd lost the battle. He liked to think that he'd learned how to more graciously lose since then.

Ash nodded.

"From now on, I'm just another challenger," Leon continued. Ash was the new Champion. "I'll

have lots of battles and become even stronger!"

"Me too! I wanna have tons of battles!" Ash declared. Reaching his goal of beating Leon had not really changed him at all!

"Let's battle again sometime," Leon said, holding out his hand.

Ash laughed a little and grabbed Leon's hand. "You've got it!"

"Pika pi!" Pikachu chirped, and jumped onto Charizard's nose with a big grin.

Dawn and Chloe were smiling at the door. "It's getting to be about time for the awards ceremony!" Dawn reminded them.

It wasn't long before Ash and Leon were back on the arena floor. Ash was on a platform, surrounded by his team of Pokémon: Pikachu, Gengar, Dragonite, Dracovish, Lucario, and Sirfetch'd.

The announcer summed up the tournament. *"With this gathering of Champions from all over the world, the Pokémon World Coronation Series Masters Eight Tournament presents the best in exciting battling!"* he said. *"And now, Leon will present the trophy to our newest Champion, Ash Ketchum!"*

The crowd went wild. Leon carried the huge, gleaming trophy cup over and placed it in Ash's hands—and Gengar grabbed it away and hoisted it in the air! Then the rest of Ash's team crowded in for a big, happy hug. They had really done it. They were all World Coronation Series Champions!

Back in Pallet Town, Ash's other Pokémon were overcome with emotion. They were blasting water, fire, and whirlwinds of leaves into the air in celebration. Torkoal was crying tears of happiness, and Totodile and Oshawott could not stop jumping for joy!

"A welcome sight of celebration and fireworks!" Professor Oak said, watching the Pokémon create a festive display.

Delia smiled. "And the grateful feelings of a mother to the friends cheering on her son back home."

And in the luxury boxes high above the stadium floor, Diantha looked at Cynthia and said, "You know, I've suddenly gotten the urge to have a battle."

"Great! Me too!" Cynthia replied. "I'm free." The two members of the Masters Eight laughed as if they were kids again.

Despite his big brother's loss, Hop acknowledged the fact that Ash had fought well. Sonia was happy that both her friends had had a good battle.

"Great, Ash! You did it!" Dawn cheered for her old friend.

"Congratulations!" added Chloe.

Team Rocket joined the cheering. "Yes! Our Pikachu comes shining through!" Jesse said with glee.

"Though I feel like something slipped our minds . . ." James admitted. He'd forgotten their devious plan to steal all the most powerful Pokémon from the tournament venue. It was no wonder—the finals had been mind-blowing! They were enough to distract even the most evil of villains, and Team Rocket hardly qualified as that.

"All right!" Ash cheered once he was finally done posing for pictures.

"Pikaaaaa!" his most loyal partner chirped from his shoulder.

He was officially the world's strongest Trainer!

It was hard to believe that every battle over the last year had been building to that point. It had been quite a journey! Ash had achieved his goal: to defeat Leon. Looking around the stadium full of cheering fans, Ash wondered if he now felt complete. Was this as rewarding as he had always dreamed it would be?

That night, as Ash was drifting off to sleep, he remembered that he had had another goal—almost from the very start. Before he had even met Leon or seen him battle, Ash had set his sights on becoming a Pokémon Master. That was a goal that would be harder to achieve than becoming the reigning Monarch. The path to being a Pokémon Master didn't have clear-cut tournament brackets and levels. You didn't receive a trophy at the end. Still, Ash believed it was a worthy goal. Was pursuing that his next step?

After a deep, satisfying night of sleep, Ash woke to his phone chanting at him: *You have a call from Goh. You have a call from Goh.*

"Pikachu! I'm sure it's about Mew!" Ash yelled out.

He grabbed his phone as fast as he could. "Hey, Goh. What's up?"

Pikachu and Ash were excited to hear about Goh's adventure. After all, the journey is the best part—and it's even better when it's shared with friends.